The Dead Follow

THE DEAD
FOLLOW
True Stories of
Supernatural Encounters

OSCAR MENDOZA

Acknowledgment

My first book, *The Book of the Dead*, was an introduction into my haunted past. In many ways, it was a catalyst into a new paranormal world I never knew existed. My new book, *The Dead Follow*, has been a completely different experience overall – as a writer and as a medium. I would go even further and call it an evolution in writing and development of psychic abilities.

I would like to start by dedicating this book to my family and friends. First, my skeptical wife Lupe. Even though she *has* experienced the paranormal with me, she keeps me grounded. My kids, Olivia and Ronin, also share my gift to see the dead. Hopefully, one day, they will share their ghost stories with the world; life wouldn't be worth living without you guys. To my brother Juan who has been with me throughout my dark, tormented life. I would love for him to tell his ghost stories. To my little brother Edgar, who is my partner in crime and best friend. My sister Vivian, who I truly love for her constant support, for being the most emotionally sensitive, and keeping all of my family grounded. To my parents for all their love and support in anything I do. To my brother-in-law Gonzo for being my biggest fan, and my cousin, Mando, for always being there when I needed him. To my fraternity brother Odet, who always believed in me. I have so many people to thank, especially my editor and good friend Cindy Brumley, who is my mentor and an inspiration. Hopefully, she will write my biography and explore my philosophy and dark past with the otherworld.

As I venture deeper into the darkness, I know the light of hope and prayers from family and friends will help guide and protect me from the evil that awaits me, as I cross through the veil into the unknown and beyond. Only the true believers will follow me into the madness. The madness is what I know and offer.

About the Author

Oscar Mendoza was born in Dallas, Texas and attended public school in Oak Cliff. He also attended St. Mary's University where he joined Lambda Chi Alpha fraternity in San Antonio, Texas and graduated with a BA. After graduation, he moved back to his hometown of Oak Cliff where he later attended Texas A & M University, in Commerce, Texas, for his MBA.

CONTENTS

Public Service Announcement

Sometimes I wish I could turn off this curse. I am not just a magnet for the dead, but other nastier non-human spirits that visit me at night. These are what religious types would call *djinn* (*jinn*) or demons. What's the difference between a human spirit from non-human one you ask? It may be easier to describe the differences as what they are *not*.

Human spirits are not as powerful because they require so much energy to do anything in the physical world. They're the ones that drain the physical, emotional, and mental batteries of a living human. The human spirit cannot mimic, but often manifest during holidays and in places they occupied before dying. A human spirit can attach itself to you and follow you anywhere, unlike the non-human. Another characteristic is that they can make noises like footsteps, or whisper in your ear, can reflect or appear in windows and glass, move objects, or close doors and cabinets.

A non-human entity is wholly evil, stronger, and can physically hurt you. The non-human can mimic animals and people, like young children, to gain your trust. Unlike a human spirit, they must be invited into your house via a spirit-summoning tool, for example: Ouija board, tarot cards, spells, scary movies, Internet, and occult books. The non-human haunt natural open areas like forests or valleys. They leave physical evidence of their presence (in the form of bruises and scratches on living things), destroy property, emit rotten smells of decay – which attract insects, and create cold spots. Non-human spirits envy the living and will do anything to consume a person's life force, if given a chance.

Have you ever felt exhausted after visiting a haunted location? Have you gone about your day and become upset for no reason at all? Have you ever become tired or confused for no explainable reason? It is possible your life energy drained by something evil, thus causing weakness. These spirits can also hold you down while you sleep causing sleep paralysis. They can hide in your closet, or in crawl spaces, or under the bed, or in bathrooms. Even worse, these non-human things feed off fear and will haunt your dreams – *if* you have invited them.

How could you protect yourself from the paranormal, you ask?

Just follow these three simple rules, well, maybe four:

1. Don't visit haunted locations, don't watch shows or movies based on ghosts, and don't read true ghost stories after midnight.

2. Don't read or watch shows based on real ghost stories in front of a mirror or after midnight.

3. Don't repeat the names of the ghosts you read in stories or hear in movies. You might inadvertently invite them into your house.

4. Whatever you do, do *not* play with a Ouija board or any other spirit-summoning game.

This book continues the sampling of paranormal events of me and my family during my teenage and young adult years. The stories are real and interwoven with childhood references. Enjoy my stories, but heed the rules.

INTRODUCTION
Life as a Teenage Psychic Medium in the Age of Gangster Rap.

I FEEL IT'S IMPORTANT to give background information about my teenage years. Cultural differences influenced my thoughts and behaviors during the daily struggles of school and home, as you will soon learn. In the early nineties in South Dallas, N.W.A. and gangster rap was all the rage in the ghetto. So were high top fades, big hair, polo shirts, and polo boots – all elements of the hottest fashions.

The city council had abandoned Oak Cliff a long time ago. Why would they care? My neighborhood had "gotten rotten" with urban decay due to the onslaught of gang violence and neglect of our streets by the city. Drugs and hookers saturated downtown Oak Cliff, while the violence between rival gangs and police had reached a level not seen in Dallas since the Prohibition Era. Random shootings were part of everyday life. Compounding the matter was that a serial killer was on the loose, preying on hookers in Oak Cliff.

Even though death was nothing new in my neighborhood, this wasn't a stellar time to be an inner-city teen. The smell of burnt exhaust and noise was a constant reminder of where I lived. The sound of the "ghetto bird" hummed overhead during nightly raids; its spotlight shined through our windows and in our yards. If you don't know the meaning of "ghetto bird," it's a police helicopter. You couldn't wear anything that looked gang-related, like reds, blues, or certain shoes. Stupid mistakes like that would surely get you killed. It sounds crazy, but it was our reality. *La Muerte*, Lady Death, was all around us, especially our schools, and there was no stopping her. I could count many friends lost just by shooting drive-byes and random acts of gang brutality. The violence had reached a zenith, stress fracturing the city, and it was about to break Dallas in half.

The Dallas School District, to remedy the gang crisis, was among the first public schools in the nation to install metal detectors. My school had its own police gang unit on campus. Life during the age of gangster rap in South Dallas was dangerous, especially if you're different. Either you're "gang-related" or a "wannabe." Regardless, we all matched the description: Mexican with brown skin and a high top fade; and this was per the officers stationed at our school. I didn't blame them, since many of these officers were very young and Caucasian. The kids would give the officers names based on their distinct personality, like "Pacman," "Robocop," and other less than pleasant names.

One can become accustomed to misery and depression and not all suffering is equal. The dead were all around and they wanted my attention. As I lived in a paranormal-filled world, in the heart of the ghetto, these are my true ghost stories.

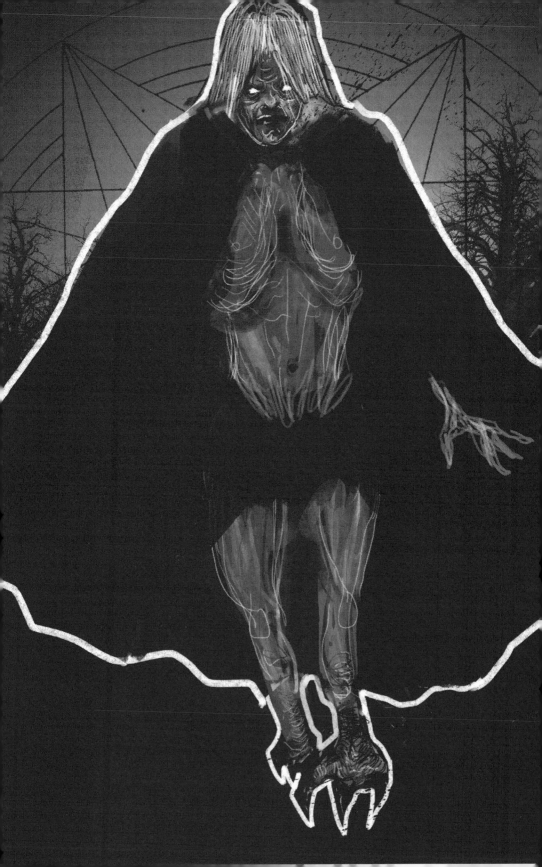

CHAPTER 1
Don't Look Up (1967)

M Y FATHER, JUST like me, can see the dead. Whether we're together or when I'm alone, it doesn't matter, the dead always follow us. In many cases, anyone who spends enough time with me may also see and experience the paranormal. I'm not sure if it's because of my abilities, but my father had the same problem when he was a kid.

The year was 1967, and my dad, Juan, was eleven years old. He and Miguel, a friend, had gone to see a late movie. The *Wizard of Oz* was playing in the only theater in town. It had gotten late, but lucky for them, Miguel's father, Manuel, had decided to walk them home from the movies. His old man was a trombone player in a folk band that had just played at the plaza. Since Manuel was already in the area, he decided to wait for the boys after the film ended. Manuel was a tall man of 6' 5," so he towered over both boys. It was getting dark and too dangerous to be in the streets. His father decided to take a shortcut through an old historic road called Cinco de Mayo Street, a mostly vacant tract of land surrounded by abandoned homes with shattered windows. San Felipe, in Mexico, had fallen on hard times, thus the widespread disrepair and vandalism. In the past, the neighborhood had been full of mansions owned by wealthy landowners back in the revolutionary days, before Poncho Villa and the Mexican revolution had taken place.

The area around Cinco de Mayo Street is known to be haunted, due to its tragic past. Multiple unsolved murders and brutal battles between soldiers and revolutionaries had taken place here. The area was also known to be haunted by the woman in white, so local kids avoided walking alone on this avenue after dark. Located next to the main plaza in the center of San Felipe, it's a busy street during the day, but at night, was a different story.

Juan felt safe with his friend's old man; the boys stayed close to his side. Like most streets back in the day, there were no streetlights. The road became extremely dark, especially on Cinco de Mayo. As they walked the sidewalk of Cinco de Mayo, they noticed an oppressive shadow. It seemed to follow them as they moved through the darkness.

The wind started to pick up and a strange *swoosh* came from above their heads. Juan swore he felt fingers touch his hair as he ducked. They heard the odd *swoosh* again, coming closer and closer, and this time he felt fingers race through his hair, as he ducked. Both boys quickly huddled closer to Manuel as he stopped and looked around. Juan's first thought it was that it was a bird or a bat, since they're common in this area, but that wasn't the case. Whatever creature had been airborne, suddenly melted into the shadows when they stopped in their tracks to look around.

"Did you see that?" Manuel called the boys.

Abruptly, an unknown voice called out, "Juan," and was followed by another *swoosh*. Then another voice from a different direction called out, "Juan," again. Miguel's dad turned pale as he spotted something in the darkness; he looked terrified. Juan had seen this look before when his little sister was afraid of a circus clown. This expression of terror continued to frighten the boys as Manuel tried to identify what he has seen.

Quickly, he put his arms around both boys, and whispered to them, "Whatever you do, don't look up." A filmy white sheet passed over their heads and landed a couple of feet in front of them. "Don't look, please, close your eyes," as they both complied. Manuel started to walk faster, turning around and guiding them in the opposite direction. "Move boys, faster, faster," Manuel begged them to hurry up. Juan tripped as he tumbled to the ground. Manuel's strong hand pulled him up, then grabbed the collars of both boys. Miguel was worried by his papa's odd demeanor. Juan had never seen such a frightened man before; that worried him.

'What can scare such a big man?' Juan pondered, as he slowly opened his eyes. For an instant, he saw two white feet attached to a slender woman's body, covered by the white sheet, which had flown above their heads. It was unbelievable what he was witnessing. He tried to comprehend with his 11-year-old logic, but nothing he told himself made sense. He had just finished watching the *Wizard of Oz*, so it had to be a witch.

'So is it a witch? What other explanation can there be?' he asked himself. The witch seemed to float weightlessly through the air in their direction.

"Don't look at her," commanded Manuel. He quickly covering Juan's eyes after noticing he was looking at the odd spectacle.

Manuel murmured under his breath, "*Lechuza.*" Juan had heard this word before. His mother described an encounter with a *lechuza* when she was a young woman. She described the *lechuza* as a half-bird, half-woman that calls out your name before it eats you. Juan instantly felt fingers graze his forehead again. Manuel told the boys to duck and run since they could run faster than Manuel could move.

"Juan," the voice called out again from behind them. It was the voice of the *lechuza* and it sounded like an owl, but it was clearly saying his name. "Juan," said the voice again, but this time from a distance. The woman in the white sheet landed directly in front of their path to cut them off. The sensation of this heavy, non-human creature hit the ground so hard that Manuel stepped back.

"Don't look. Let's go this way, quickly," commanded Manuel, as he pulled the boys again in the opposite direction. Juan closed his eyes again when he realized his friend's father was right. "Hurry, don't look back. Hurry," Manuel whispered to the boys. The trio ran straight to the plaza church. Manuel ran up the steps and tried to open the doors. He knocked like a crazed man, but no one answered.

"Let us in, let us in, the *lechuza* is trying to get my kids," he called out. He looked around but saw no one. Manuel made the sign of the cross over his chest and figured they were safe for the time being. "Let's keep walking," he told the boys. They stopped to catch their breath by the steps of the church. That's when they heard a faint sobbing of a woman crying from a distance.

"My kids, where are my kids?" the woman cried.

"Run!" Manuel screamed. "Don't look back," he demanded, "She's still behind us." They took the long way to run home and never looked back. Manuel walked Juan home and waited for him to step into his house, as he spoke to his mother.

Juan's mother prayed over her son while he slept at her feet. Juan never asked his friend's father what he had seen and why he couldn't look at the woman. But deep inside, he didn't want to know.

Later that year, Manuel mysteriously died in his sleep from a heart attack. So if you ever hear your name called out at night, don't look up. If you do, you might see the *lechuza*; if you do see her, you'd better run. If you don't, she will eat you.

CHAPTER 2
The Sobbing Man (1972)

A MONTH BEFORE HE was married, Juan, my father, had seen an apparition of a man on the second floor of his father's house. Juan's older sister, Malena, also lived in the same house with her three kids. Richard, Olga, and Fernando, nicknamed Flaco, lived in the downstairs room with their mother. The house was a hacienda-style structure with an open roof design. There was one restroom and it was on the first floor. Two of the bedrooms were located at the front of the building. A third bedroom was on the second floor, the only room, having a single window facing the stairs that led to the kitchen.

Juan had to stay on the second floor because there was no more room. Since he moved upstairs, he hadn't had a good night of sleep. No one wanted to sleep in that room because it was haunted. Every night, at 2 o'clock in the morning, an unknown man would walk up to his room, open the door, and sit next to him while he slept. The man sobbed all night long. Juan would feel the weight of the man on his bed. He remained silent, never dared to look, and made sure not to move a muscle for fear the stranger would notice him. Juan was fed up because he had endured this entity for far too long. He didn't want to sleep in this room anymore, but he didn't have any other choices.

This particular night, he decided to take five-year-old Flaco to stay upstairs with him. After Juan made up the bed, he placed the kid next to the wall. Juan would make sure if anything came that night he would be the first to see it. Midnight quickly came and Juan's eyes got heavy; it was way past Flaco's bedtime. In those days, families went to bed at around 8:00 p.m. after having hot tea and sweet bread.

Juan needed to awaken early the next day. He had a special day planned for Concha, his fiancé. As he was dozing off, he heard something coming up the stairs toward the second floor. The cadence of loose, open-toed sandals made its way up the stairs toward his room. Juan instantly regretted involving his young nephew; the situation could become dangerous for both. He was not sure what the spirit wanted or why it came to visit him. The strange wheezing, gurgling, and wailing sound followed by the shuffling sound of *flip-flop, flip-flop*, made his skin crawl. Juan knew *his* father didn't own sandals, and the other kids were asleep downstairs with their drunken mother. So who was the person walking up the stairs? Juan didn't want to look, so he hid underneath the sheets and hoped the man would just leave.

That's when he heard the wooden door slowly *kreeen* open and *wumph*, as it closed. The intruder was now in the room with him and his nephew. Juan felt it come close to him. He could see an outline of legs from underneath the covers. He heard it slowly trudge his way toward the wall next to the window. It looked like a man wearing weathered brown pants with patches over the right knee. He didn't dare to lift the sheets to see more, since the man could have easily grabbed him at any time.

The heavy presence continued to cross the room slowly, like a python sizing up its prey. The slow *flip-flop, flip-flop, flip-flop* of steps rang in Juan's ears, as he grabbed onto his sleeping nephew. Juan was compelled get a glimpse of the specter. The intruder now stood next to the window by the corner of the bed. Juan tucked his feet closer to his body, in case the stranger tried to grab his foot. After what seemed like a long time, Juan somehow knew it – whatever it was – wasn't going to take him or his nephew; he concluded that the entity's energy was not threating. Casting aside his fears, he gazed at the sobbing man. The stranger covered his face with both hands as he cried. From what Juan could tell, the intruder had long, black hair with bits of dirt and other debris from dirt roads, like grass and pebbles. The stench of this dead person was overwhelming his senses. Before he could stop himself, the words poured out of his mouth.

"Can I help you?" Juan asked, instantly regretting his words. By acknowledging the dead, he had given invitation for interaction – and he couldn't rescind the offer. The man stopped sobbing for a second and slowly put down his hands.

He responded, "You see me." With both arms extended in a threatening gesture, he started to move toward Juan. That was when Juan saw the man's face was missing his nose and parts of his lower jaw, exposing a swollen, hanging tongue. His eyes seemed to glow pure white. As the ghost moved toward Juan again, the stranger's tongue wagged up and down trying to talk, but only gibberish came out. The wheezing got louder as Juan realized he was hearing air escaping through a hole in the man's neck. Juan couldn't move anymore; he was frozen. He then made up his mind to confront the mutilated corpse.

"What do you want with me?" Juan asked, standing his ground while holding onto his nephew.

"*No me tengas miedo*," "Don't be scared," said the broken voice. The mutilated body floated across the room without moving its legs, its arms still extended toward him.

'Look away, look away. Don't show it fear,' Juan told himself. But he couldn't move, as though an unknown force had locked his head in place. As it floated closer to him, the glowing, white marble eyes were the only thing visible. Whatever the man wanted, Juan couldn't stop him; he was at his mercy now. He closed his eyes and waited for his fate.

The ghoul stopped next to Juan, slowly leaned over him, and placed a mummified hand on his chest, whispering, "*Es la casa*," "It's the house."

Terrified and spent, Juan passed out, falling into a deep sleep. He slept for what seemed to be minutes, but upon waking, realized the room had become brighter and it was now daytime. He quickly checked his body for bites or bruises - nothing. Next, he made sure

Flaco was okay. He quickly picked up the child and ran downstairs to tell his father what had happened.

Juan found his father in the kitchen drinking coffee and eating breakfast. He began explaining what happened to his father. Don Rafael didn't have time for nonsense and brushed it aside. He told Juan to grow up and be a man if he wanted to marry Concha.

"Only children believe in ghosts. What are you, a child or a man?" Don Rafael screamed at him. Juan didn't care, he knew what he witnessed. There was something familiar about the dead man. The ghost wanted to tell him something, 'What about the house? Could it have been a warning?' he wondered. It wasn't the first time the dead talked to him, but this was different. This was the first time the dead didn't want to hurt him and Juan knew he was a good spirit. He didn't encounter the sobbing man after that night. Embarrassed for being scared, Juan never mentioned his encounter to Concha, and he only told me many years later. It turned out that it was a warning to Juan, but he wouldn't find out until it was too late.

I, too, have a history with this house. This was the same house, where I saw the zombie ghost clown.

CHAPTER 3
The Dead Follow (1973)
Part I: The Curse

MANY CULTURES ACROSS the world believe in curses, except for me. I didn't believe in such superstitions at the time, because I found them to be far-fetched. That is, until my father told me about our family curse. Far-fetched manifested as a reality when I experienced the curse for myself. I traced the evil back to my paternal grandfather's first marriage. The darkness itself had taken a toll on his mind, as the hex slowly soured my grandfather's soul - to the point he became violent. Rafael wasn't always a mean, hateful man.

The trouble started when Rafael met a beautiful young woman named Maria. As a young man, he already had a reputation of being a womanizer. Don Rafael was a smooth talker and handsome man, even at the age of 40. I remember looking at his pictures when he was a young man. He reminded me of a famous, classic Mexican actor, from Mexico's golden age, by the name of Pedro Infante. Don Rafael was a dead ringer for Pedro, and I'm sure people confused him with the actor. Don Rafael had naturally broad shoulders, a classic muscular build, and a well-trimmed mustache. He had married into money and, by his own right, ran a successful carpet business with his family.

Rafael fell madly in love with Maria, who was quite young at the time. Maria's mother did not approve of their love affair. Rafael convinced Maria to run away to San Felipe, Mexico. Maria had been born near San Antonio, Texas, so she was an American citizen who was visiting. Rafael had just abandoned his first wife and several children for Maria.

If you haven't guessed it, Maria is my grandmother, my dad's mom. At some point, we believe that my paternal grandfather's first wife had a curse put on Rafael *and* Maria. Regardless of who initiated the curse, it was placed on both of them, by a family member.

I am sure you're wondering what the curse was and what happens when one is cursed. According to my father, the dead follow us around. Ever since my father was a small child, the dead visit him at night, talk to him, and sometimes have aggressively attacked him. To this day, he is regularly haunted and stalked by a witch.

"Remember, the dead follow us," he warned me, knowing I too, had inherited my grandfather's curse. He told me that a *nagual* had bound to our family and now we were part of this entity. A *nagual* is a witch or demon that can become an animal by wearing the animal's skin. This is similar to the Native American Indian skin-walker, except *naguals*, are more like werewolves, only able to transform at night during a full moon.

Sounds crazy, right? But there is much truth to what he told me. I believe that hate – a raw, venomous hatred, can take form and manifest into something real. This hate-filled entity follows us until we die and at the end, comes for us in the form of the *nagual*. I was told that right after my grandmother died, a big black dog appeared in front of her house and followed her remains to the cemetery. I thought it was just an ordinary dog at first, until my grandfather died four years later. Then I, too, witnessed the big black dog.

This wouldn't be the last time I saw the *nagual* again. I believe this is the reason I can see the dead and the dead sometimes attack me in my sleep. Curses are real and be taken seriously. If you're ever cursed, the dead will follow you until your last day on this earth. You will never have a restful sleep or genuinely enjoy life because the undead will always make sure they are around you.

The Dead Follow (1973)
Part 2: Juan and Concha

LIFE FOR MY parents in rural Mexico was unforgiving, especially for a newly married couple. Compounded by the paranormal, life for them became unbearable. My father, Juan, had married the love of his life, Concha, in a quiet ceremony under their favorite tree in the town square plaza. He didn't have enough money to afford a proper wedding. Concha didn't care. At the time, Juan worked for his father, Don Rafael, making little to no money; but he had promised his heart, and that was enough for Concha.

Concha was a petit, beautiful woman with long black hair and fair skin. Juan thought of her as his princess. Like his father Don Rafael, Juan was handsome, blessed with muscular, broad shoulders, a full chest, and wore the classic razor-thin, Latino mustache. He, too, was considered a womanizer and Concha's family had warned her to stay away from him. But unlike Don Rafael, his heart belonged to one woman, Concha. She didn't care what her family thought; she loved him with all her heart.

They had met years before when Concha worked in the market square selling roasted chickens. He would stop on his way to work and flirt with her as she prepared the birds. Secretly, Juan loved the smell of roasted chicken because it reminded him of his crush. Every day, he made it a point to walk to work a bit earlier than usual, just to talk to her. They both lived on the same street near the enormous Indian statue that divided the neighborhood, so it was always easy to see her working outside her house. He had loved her from a distance until he finally had the guts to confess his feelings.

Juan had always felt a deep connection with her, but couldn't explain the attraction. Concha also had similar feelings for her handsome neighbor down the street. After two years of dating, their relationship blossomed into an engagement. They were young and full of life and dreamed of a better future in America. Juan worked with his father in construction, but would give up his own life to make Concha happy – this is when the paranormal activity began.

Juan and Concha had just been married only a couple of months when the haunting started. At a young age, he could see and speak to the dead. Concha had her own abilities as a powerful empath and psychic. As a young child, she could see people's auras and feel their pain. One of the extraordinary abilities Concha has is foretelling the future in her dreams. Rumors say she inherited her gifts from her grandmother, who was a powerful witch. Juan was used to experiencing the paranormal on his own, but that would change when he married Concha. It was almost if Concha amplified their abilities – for the worse. Their union had awoken the Mendoza curse, and like a wound that wouldn't heal, it began to fester.

Life wasn't as cheerful as they had hoped for. As soon as Concha moved into Juan's parents' house, an unknown presence began to affect the health of both Concha and Juan. This strange illness fell upon her, causing her to lose weight. She was already thin, but now she looked emaciated. Concha had become a shell of her formal self, because of a constant fever, leaving her bed-ridden for months. The medical experts had no reason for the ailment or how to properly treat her condition, which they blamed on depression and the pressure of being married, but Concha knew better. She could feel the energy escape from her body, as if an unseen parasite fed on her while she slept.

'It's the house. It's evil,' Concha intuited, as she lied in bed. Drained, she tried to be strong for her husband. It was bad enough that her husband's family hated her for marrying Juan but now Concha had to deal with an evil entity.

Concha tried to protect herself with charms and the rituals, but nothing helped; this energy wasn't human. The entity felt disgusting to her as her skin reacted to the sensation. She knew the spirit belonged to an evil and unnatural beast.

Finally, Concha recognized a pattern. The evil energy only attacked her when her husband was around. It was almost as if the evil spirit didn't want them together. Juan had found a job in Texas working with his uncle and soon left Concha behind with his family. The instant Juan left for America, the fever lifted and her body became normal. Concha had constructed a theory that whatever was attacking her was attached to her husband and it only manifested in this house.

She hated living there and began to resent him for leaving her behind to suffer in this hell. Too much negative energy had consumed her body to the point she needed to escape outside. His family didn't help, as his sisters criticized her constantly, gave her the evil eye, called her names and accused her of things in which she was not involved. If there was a hell on earth, she felt she was in it. The only upside was that her parents lived down the street, so she made it a point to visit her family as much as she could. She needed to find a way out without insulting his parents. She reminded herself what her husband gave up for her, so she had to be brave for both of them. Unbelievably, she would rather have dealt with the undead than Juan's family.

Nights before, Concha had foreseen in a dream a hideous devil and an infant. In her nightmare, the demon wanted to eat the young child. She held the child in her arms and ran, but the devil was always behind her, lurking in the darkness. This dream frightened her to the core, so much so that she mentioned it to her mother.

"Beware, something is coming for you, daughter," her mother warned her. Usually dreams pose riddles, but this one was too specific, felt too real, and made her cry.

Juan promised her she would only have to stay with his parents for a little while. As soon as he had enough money, he would send for her. Months became two years, and Concha started to lose faith that her husband would keep his promise.

Loneliness led to doubt, as she questioned their relationship, now finding herself pregnant. With the pregnancy, a different wave of nightly demonic attacks began without Juan being present. Before, the entity left her alone when he went back to America, now things had changed. The new evil presence focused its attention on the unborn child in her belly. It almost seemed as though her baby had inherited the curse. Concha isolated herself in her room and patiently waited for her husband to come back home.

There is no one more dangerous than a desperate mother trying to protect her child. She would no longer be a victim – nothing else mattered. Concha, instead of trying to protect *herself*, contrived a plan to defend her room instead. She lit holy candles and blessed the space with holy water. She sealed the door with sea salt, because she had heard salt protects dwellings from harmful spirits. Now nothing unholy could come into her room. There had been no paranormal activity for several months; her plan worked.

The following evening started as an ordinary night. Juan had just gone back to America and she felt even lonelier as her baby moved in her belly. Concha was so tired she had forgotten to light her protection candle. Hours passed as she fell into a deep sleep; a noise woke her abruptly. Because of the advancing pregnancy, her back hurt and her feet were swollen, so it was hard to get out of bed. She turned her head towards the familiar sound of an unknown person walking upstairs. It couldn't be Juan's sister, as this sounded heavier, like a man. She had listened to her father-in-law walk the stairs many times, but this wasn't him. Don Rafael had gone to America with his two younger daughters, leaving Juan's older sister behind with her kids.

She protectively grabbed her swollen abdomen as her heart pounded out of her chest. Concha had a horrible feeling that made her skin crawl. She realized she had forgotten to light her candles and lock the door. The stranger continued to make his way to her room. Her mind wanted to run, but her body was too tired as she stumbled. She had no hope of locking the door before he got to her room. It was the entity again, and she knew it. The room was too dark to find a match in time. The risk of her tripping was also high. She didn't want to hurt herself trying to get to the light switch. Concha was too slow to prevent the evil spirit from entering the room. The only sensible thing was to sit on her bed and hold her rosary beads, hoping someone would come to her rescue.

She was trapped in her room and at the mercy of the beast. The unholy creature stopped in front of her door. She could hear the demon's long, deep, raspy breaths as it now stood there motionless. Concha noticed an animal-like shadow from underneath the door. Though she couldn't light a candle, she still had the sea salt barrier.

A strong force started to slam itself against the door as the hinges rattled from the impact. *Knock-knock*! *Knock-knock*! The loud noise seemed to generate from the very air in the room. Suddenly the sound of clawing came from the other side of the door, making her teeth vibrate as the sound became unbearable. Concha tried to cover her ears but it didn't help. The thing wanted in and it was willing to break the door down to get into her room.

"Stop! Stop! I command you!" she screamed. The sound of a screaming cat emanated from the stranger. *Knock-knock*! *Knock-knock*! The door finally gave in, slowly opening midway. She closed her eyes and lie back in bed. Whatever it was, was about to enter her room, so she pretended to be asleep; playing possum was her only option. She desperately prayed to God for help, "Save my baby, please Jesus. I don't care about me. Don't let the demon eat my baby." Now the sound of screaming filled the inside of her room and under the bed.

Creeeeeak, the door slowly began to open. She quickly closed her eyes out of instinct and fear. A familiar odor of cigar and whiskey filled the room. She recognized the scent from the neighborhood boys who smoked around *her* parents' house but couldn't match the smell.

Her old friend, Oscar, liked to indulge in unfiltered cigarettes when she worked in the market. They would chat off and on and soon became good friends. Oscar had a crush on her and brought her flowers throughout the day; he wasn't her type. He was a tall, thin man, with dark brown eyes, who dreamed of performing in the circus. She had not seen nor heard from him ever since he left to join the local carnival. He had promised her he would be back for her when he was rich. Concha just smiled and gave him a goodbye hug. Like most young men his age who decided to leave San Felipe, he never came back. She had no idea what happened to him. A year later, Juan came into her life.

'This isn't the time to reminisce about old boyfriends,' she thought, as the reality had become a nightmare.

"I am here, love," as the man whispered into the room, "I finally found you." She could sense it was a younger man about the age of her husband. Her instinct told her not to open her eyes, as she didn't want to see his face.

"You're not my husband," she replied. The man's mouth got so close to her ear, she felt his breath on her neck.

"I can save you, *mi amor*," he answered, picking Concha up. His biceps were as hard as the cement bags her father used to repair his house. The fingers grasped her hips and cradled her, oh so gently, carrying her outside into the night.

Concha was frozen, not able to scream or fight back, tears streaked down her face. The beast was taking her and her unborn baby away, to God knew where. Her eyes slowly opened to see the stars and the streetlight as the entity floated them down the street, its feet seemingly hanging in mid-air. A soothing light engulfed her as a sense of warmth covered both the stranger and her. She wasn't afraid anymore. Whoever, or whatever it was, didn't want to hurt her, because of the way he carried her.

'Stay calm and wait for your moment,' she told herself. The stranger finally stopped and set her gently on the steps of the Catholic Church.

"I will save you and your son," the man whispered one last time in her ear. The cold wind hit her bare skin and a shiver ran down her spine. Concha realized she was only wearing her nightgown. She sat there confused as the man disappeared inside the church. Should she run or wait for the stranger? Concha felt safe, even though circumstances scared her.

The stranger reappeared and picked her up again, carrying her back through the street as black felines surrounded them. The enormous cat-like beasts were not average-sized cats, but much larger. They hissed, meowed, and clawed at her feet, but the angel-like man shielded her from the animal's attacks. The stranger laid her gently again in front of her house. Then he stood guard against the demonic felines that followed and still surrounded both of them. Concha kept her eyes averted from his face, but something told her to peek. She slowly opened her eyes.

'Just one quick look,' she told herself. At the last minute, she raised her head to look at the man, but instead, didn't have the nerve to follow through. Instead, she looked downward and noticed he was wearing old overalls covered in dirt. Concha recognized them and wanted to call out the man's name.

Before she could say anything, the voice whispered, "You need to leave this house. Now sleep." Her eyes became heavy and she fell asleep.

Concha woke up as the sun lifted from behind her. She found herself outside the door to the house. Her back ached as she slowly got up and waddled back to her bedroom. Could this have been a dream? Deep inside, she knew it wasn't.

The next day she called Juan, who was still in America, about the man's warning. When he returned, things got worse as both fell ill again from the same unknown ailment. The following nights, the clawing sounds of cats surrounded their room; the unholy felines attacked the door again, and again. They would hear chains falling down the stairs and footsteps of a man walking up and down the stairs. Concha reminded Juan of the stranger's warning. Juan had no choice; he finally took his wife to America. The night before they left for Texas – whatever the negative energy was – was not as happy. They both heard it stomping outside the door, as if waiting for them to fall asleep.

All the paranormal activity stopped in his parents' house, once he took Concha to Texas. However, a new nightmare was about to begin after they moved into the apartment complex on Bishop Street.

Soon after my brother, Juan Jr., was born in Dallas, Concha found out she was expecting again, attracting a *new* paranormal entity. Concha called the beast the smiling man. It too, wanted the baby in her belly, but this time there wasn't an angel to protect her. After the baby was born, the smiling man focused all its attention on her new baby, Oscar. Her newborn innocently attracted the undead and Concha's new battle was to deal with the smiling man.

Oscar was born with a bloody veil, also known as a caul, and a circular red birthmark on his forehead. According to Concha's mother, as well as what many cultures believe, being born with a veil signifies uniqueness in a child. Unbeknownst to Concha, Oscar had inherited both his parents' abilities and the Mendoza curse.

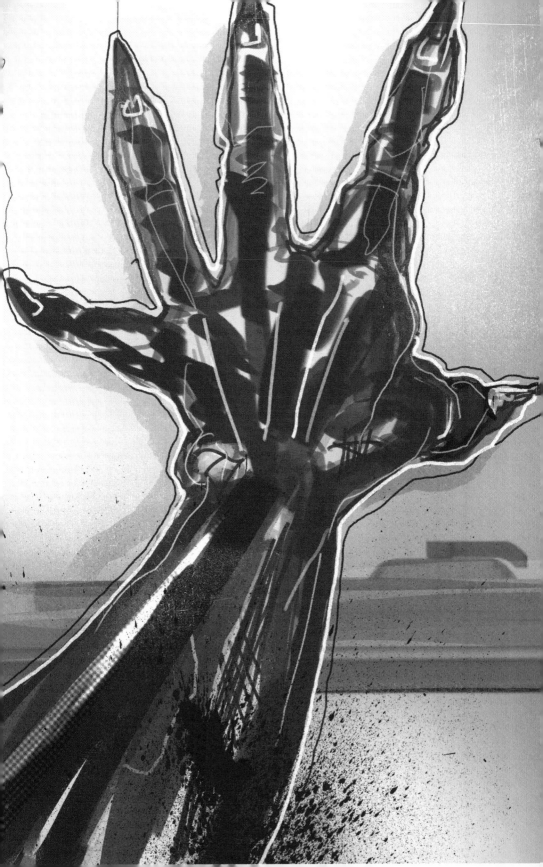

CHAPTER 4
It Came from the Crawl Space (1993)

Spring in Texas is beautiful, and this is the only time of the year when the weather in Texas was perfect, in my not so humble teenage opinion. Unlike the weather, my grades suffered from tardiness and absences because of oversleeping and nightly adventures. As luck would have it, attending summer school gave me an excuse to skip the annual vacation to Mexico. By this point, I was tired of trips to San Felipe, plus my newly attained social status allowed me to go to all high school parties. I had become too busy to join my parents on vacation. I wanted to take the time to reflect on my future, or lack thereof, with Shelly. Our relationship was starting to change and I could feel the end approaching.

My brother and I spent most of our time staying at our house with my Uncle Coco or my paternal grandparents' house, who had years before also moved to Dallas. Their house was about two blocks down the street from our home in Oak Cliff and had its own personality. It was an old, run-of-the-mill, brick home painted bright yellow with a beautiful rose garden and a Virgin Mary statue in the front, all of it surrounded by an old, broken, chain link fence. The layout consisted of a living room, kitchen, dining room, master bedroom, and a guest room. The porch was converted into a third bedroom, functioning as both second guest room and makeshift office.

My grandparents prided themselves on the beautiful terrace of rose bushes and wild herbs brought from Mexico. My grandmother, a healer, ran a small business out of her office/guest room, using these herbs and skills. She learned from her mother, who was taught by her grandmother several generations back. She was the go-to person when you injured yourself or you thought you'd been cursed. The neighborhood considered her a white witch. She was a sweet, petite woman, all of four feet and eleven inches, the average for indigenous Indians of her town in Mexico. As for grandfather, he was a strict and disciplined man who demanded his grandchildren's best behavior, always.

I especially hated their house. Oh, not because of what you may think. The house had an aura of dark energy that originated from underneath its foundation, emitting a putrid odor that only I could smell. It was like a god-awful stench of decay that had been stewing for days in the hot sun; the type that would burn the inside of your nose. I often asked my grandparents, "Is there a dead cat underneath the house?" and they would always respond, "No." The negative energy that emanated from the house raised the hairs on the back of my head every time I visited.

The dining room had a small closet used for storage. The design of this closet door gave me the creeps. It was the type of door you would find in a hundred-year-old Victorian styled house. I am sure it was original to this house since it was constructed in the eighteen hundreds. Besides looking creepy, it was heavy and hard to move because of foundation issues. This actually gave me some comfort because the door couldn't swing open by itself.

I always thought, 'What a strange place to have a closet. Why would you need a closet in the dining room? Maybe it's just an oversized pantry.' Even though it was for storage, inside was another smaller door leading to a hidden crawl space. This crawl spaced scared me to the point that I was compelled keep a constant eye on the outer door. I figured if it was big enough for a child to hide in, it was also big enough to hide a dead body, and that was reason enough to be afraid.

Every time I had dinner with my grandparents, I felt this creepy, shivery sensation like I was being watched. If I had to walk past the door,

I made sure to do it as quickly as possible. I had this overwhelming fear that a creature, from hell itself, was leering and ready to pounce out of the shadows.

Beware the Cat's Meow (1993)
Part 1: The Headless Man

My OLDER COUSIN Helen lived at my grandparents' house for many years with her mother, younger brothers, and little sister. Helen claimed something would crawl out of the storage closet and go to her bedroom every night. It would then sit next to her on the bed and stroke her hair while she slept. One time she decided to wait for the intruder to visit her as she hid under her blankets. She convinced herself she wanted to catch whoever it was. She rationalized it was her mother, Estella, even though she called it the headless man.

Estella worked the late shift at a potato-processing warehouse. Estella was a single mother, who barely made enough money to feed her four children. When the opportunity presented to work extra shifts, she jumped at the chance. This was a labor-intensive job of packaging and cutting potatoes for stores and restaurants. Helen had no idea of the working hell her mother endured. She was never able to spend time with her because she would be at school when her mother arrived home to eat, shower, and go to sleep. Helen became both older sister and stand-in mother to her youngest sibling, Maria.

Helen and Maria shared the same bed. Both were teenagers, Helen, seventeen and Maria, thirteen, and their room was still filled with teddy bears and girly things. On this particular night, Helen was listening for her sister to fall asleep, while lying next to her. Helen hid under her blankets and pretended to fall asleep while listening to favorite music on her Walkman. The room was especially dark, even though there were four large windows, all of which faced the unlit backyard.

Sometime between Michael Jackson's *Human Nature* and *Billy Jean*, she accidentally dozed off and awoke up 5 minutes 'til 3 o'clock in the morning. Helen rubbed her eyes to get her bearings and noticed a thick, white mist had formed on the floor of their room. She quickly removed her headphones.

'What the hell?' she told herself in disbelief, as she made the sign of the cross on her forehead. Out of the darkness, she heard a cat meow, another meow followed. It seemed to come from the underneath the bed. She got nervous and quickly raised the covers over her head to hide from whatever was out there. Fear overcame her because they didn't own a cat; besides, grandpa hated cats. Maybe it was her mother, she thought, so she peeked toward the door.

"Mom," she softly called out. Helen hoped her mother was playing a practical joke on her, expecting her to pop out of the other side of the door, but nothing. To her horror, she heard another cat meowing where she thought her mother would be hiding. 'How can there be cats everywhere?' she thought, trying to make sense of the situation.

A long, slow creak came from the dining room storage closet, making the hairs on her neck stand up. The sound of cats meowing filled every corner of the room. Helen recoiled in fear. She realized from the low raspy and scraping sounds that something was dragging itself from the dining room. Something or someone was slowly pulling itself forward, desperately trying to reach her room. This scared her to her core. 'Maybe it's all in my head,' she thought, as chill ran through her body. As it got closer, the *rasp, rasp, scrape* got louder, but now she could hear heavy breathing. She realized maybe it couldn't walk or see because of the way it moved.

The reality of the situation finally set in. Her survival instinct told her to run and lock the door before it reached her room. She couldn't move and didn't believe she was that brave. Her brain burned with the rush of adrenaline. She hyperventilated and trembled uncontrollably.

Rasp, rasp, scrape, as the thing continued to drag itself to her door.

'Move it! Run! Hide!' her mind begged her. But her body wouldn't respond; she was in a frozen trance. The meowing got louder and louder. The door swung open violently, as a black mass dragged itself toward her. She grabbed her sister's foot, fearing whatever it was, was going to snatch her away.

The bed slowly moved as something took hold of its wooden legs. *Thump, thud, thwack*, and *whoosh*, as the bed springs made a rattling sound. Her bed compressed and cracked as the springs bent, as if someone sat down next to her. Helen wanted to call out for help, but she feared the creature would hurt her sister.

She heard a growling type of laughter from the darkness. The meowing rang in her ears as the intruder sat next to her. The smell of decay filled her mouth and nose to the point of making her sick. The thing slowly began to stroke her head even though she was still covered with the bed sheet. Its hands felt rough and cold through the fabric. It touched her head so gently as if it were caressing a delicate flower. Somehow, her hair was catching on its loose skin.

She could feel its thick tongue-like fingers crawl over her face like a blind man would do if he wanted to know how a person looked. The hand felt cold and stone-like, but stroked like a dog's tongue. Continuing the evil wheezing giggles, his other hand began to stroke her forearm.

'Don't move,' she thought to herself. Still pretending to be asleep, she felt sweat bead on her forehead. Her stomach cramped and she trembled as she tried to hold the escaping gas. 'Hold it in,' she begged herself but the terror was too great and she lost control. The thing immediately grabbed her bicep with brutal force when it realized she was awake.

"HAVE YOU SEEN MY HEAD, SWEET CHILD?" it yelled in her ear. In one move, it jumped on top of her. Helen's back was pinned flat against the mattress, the bed sheet still between her and the stranger. She started to cry and then began to kick and scream. The bed sheet now yanked off her face, she finally got a view of her attacker. She could tell it had an older appearance because of its emaciated body. The terror she felt when she realized it was a skeletal body with no head… was gruesome beyond words. She closed her eyes, but it was too late. The image of that body without its head was forever burned into her memory.

The zombie-like thing was clothed in filthy, shredded rags. She thought that the hand still locked onto her arm belonged to that of a black man's. The ghoul had no legs, as though both had been yanked from its body by tremendous force. The neck still had bits of flesh and its spinal cord sticking out an inch from the stump that was its' neck. She noticed what looked like rice crawling all over its body.

Helen jerked and bucked as she began to gag. She felt vomit fill her throat. The chuckling got louder and louder, mockingly, as the meowing grew in volume. Tears fell from her face as the decayed hand continued to stroke her hair and cheek. She started to pray to Jesus and the Virgin Mary but nothing worked. Soon fear channeled into anger and she started to curse at the headless man. She figured if it was going to kill her she would fight back. The more she yelled, the more she could move; and suddenly, it was gone.

An unseen force had pulled the ghoul off Helen so quickly that the door slammed shut from the vacuum. Immediately, everything was quiet again. Startled, she fell off the bed but was not injured. She turned to make sure her sister was asleep and breathing and ran to her grandfather's room. He quickly got up and reached for his gun, searched her room and the dining room closet, but found nothing.

Helen and Maria ended up sleeping on the floor in their grandparents' room the rest of the night and the following week. She could not sleep in that room anymore. Helen continued to experience the headless entity over the next year but never found out what it wanted. After my cousin got married and moved out, she never spent the night at our grandparents' house anymore, only visit. Her old room was later occupied by her sister and younger brothers. She kept this story to herself until she decided to share her ghost story with us one Christmas Eve. This wouldn't be the last time my family experienced the headless man.

Beware the Cat's Meow (1993)
Part 2: Beware the Cat's Meow

THIS YEAR, MY brother and I had no choice, we had to stay at my paternal grandparents' house, and we had to sleep in the guest room. No one wanted to stay there, especially after what our cousin Helen told us about the headless man. We confronted our parents about their decision, but our fight was futile. They had already made plans for us to stay and it was final. This was all thanks to my brother's recent bad behavior. Juan had started to hang out with the wrong crowd and began to rebel against our father.

My brother and I arrived at our grandparent's home that evening while they were watching their novella. We had dinner with them and discussed our day. Grandmother showed us to the guest room, which served as her office during the day. My brother and I had to share this small room, with a queen- sized bed, having one window overlooking the front lawn.

Night arrived and my brother wanted to go out with his friends, but grandfather wouldn't let us go anywhere. We tried to use their phone to call our girlfriends, but again, my grandparents wouldn't have it. Both of us settled in for bed and talked for a while.

At this point, Juan and I had drifted apart so much I swore he hated me. He had grown rotten and despised everyone, especially me. His hatred drove me to attend a different high school. Don't get me wrong, I didn't loathe Juan. I loved my brother so I just gave him his space. I figured he had his reasons. We stopped talking at some point the year before. I can't even remember why, but it didn't matter anymore. The damage was done and now he attended Adamson High School, our local school. I attended Sunset High, which happened to be rivals with Adamson's football team.

Juan screamed, "Sleep on the floor, fool, we don't fit." I didn't want him to get his way, so I just ignored him. We both picked different spots on the bed; I selected the bottom half, he chose the upper half. I likened the room to a prison cell. The walls had wood paneling that's typical of older homes. The window had no curtains, so the street light shined into the room. I felt sick as I started thinking about my cousin's story.

'I wish I had some NyQuil,' I thought. My mother made it a point to hide NyQuil from me, because she thought I had become addicted to it. NyQuil was the only thing stopping the dead from contacting me at night. If I wanted any kind of sleep, I needed that liquid. I figured when my brother fell asleep, I'd grab his foot like I did when we were children, back when the pig man came to visit me. I had a feeling that whatever haunted my cousin would pay me a visit tonight.

In case I was attacked, the plan was to wake up my brother by pulling on his foot. I know it sounds stupid, but I felt I didn't have any other option. There is a good reason people fear the monster under the bed, because it actually exists, and yes, it/they will pull you under the bed, if possible. There was no way I was going to let the dead pull me under the bed. I tucked in my legs into the sheet to make sure I didn't get grabbed by the dead while I slept. It happened more often than I liked, so I made sure nothing could reach out to grab my feet at night. My logic, to me, was justified. After all, being a paranormal survivor, I knew what waited for me in the shadows. I've seen the beast that hides in the darkness, and it was too real to ignore. My grandmother had given me an old wooden cross for protection and I carried that cross with me everywhere. I placed the cross on the wall facing me.

Being overly cautious, I made sure all doors were closed, especially the closet. I tried to leave the lights on, but my grandfather demanded the lights be off to save on electricity. I had no choice so I turned off the lights, lie down, and grabbed my brother's foot. He was already asleep snoring away. Not me, I had a hard time closing my eyes.

I prayed to God that nothing would visit me tonight, but my prayers were not answered. I felt that God had forsaken me for some reason, but that didn't stop me from trying. It was 2 a.m. and I knew it was a matter of time before it came for me. It always did. I didn't see why anything would change, especially here. I tried to fight sleep, but fatigue got the better of me, and I closed my eyes.

I woke up abruptly around 3 a.m. to a cat meowing from the window. It wasn't strange to hear a stray cat outside, so I just moved to get comfortable. The streetlight illuminated the room enough to see in the darkness. Then I heard another cat meowing, and another. It felt like a gang of cats had gathered around the window. I tucked my feet closer to my body. I heard a clawing coming from the window. The meowing got even louder.

'What's going on?' I wondered. I woke up my brother, just to make sure he too, could listen to the clawing and meowing.

He jerked awake and asked, "What the hell is that?" The scratching sounds intensified from outside of the house and on the other side of the door. *Meow. Hiss. Meow. Hiss*, as the caterwauling surrounded us.

We heard the doorknob jiggle, as if someone was trying to open the door. Then we heard the laughter. It wasn't good laughter, but more like an evil, murderous kind; it resonated across the room. The door vibrated hard and violently as someone tried to open the door. The cat meowing became louder this time, coming from inside the room with us. We heard clawing from the outside all of the walls. A banging came from the bottom of the door. Whoever, or whatever it was, had to be lying on the floor, because we could feel the first bang on the door with a force that rattled the bottom of the doorframe. *Bang, bang, bang,* and then it stopped.

Juan whispered fearfully, "It's the headless man." We both looked around and toward the door, asking, "Did it go away?" That's when we saw the hand reaching up and claw the window. The zombie-like hand was only visible for a second, but that was long enough to see bone sticking out from its palm, its skin barely stretched over its clenched hand. The nails were not human but more like talons: white, long, and sharply pointed into a hook.

As soon as we noticed the disembodied limb, we dove under the bed sheets again. We began to pray while holding hands. A swirling, howling wind whipped around the bed. When the noise reached a crescendo, the clawing and meowing, along with the evil laughing and pounding, abruptly ceased. We both peeked before fully emerging from the sheets.

"Look," Juan demanded.

"Hell, no," I said. He checked the room and then looked out the window – everything looked normal.

"Let's go to granddad's room," he whispered.

"Hell. No. We have to pass by the storage closet." That's all I had to say to convince my brother not to open the door. Whatever it was, we knew for sure, had come from the storage closet. We decided to stay awake with our backs propped against each other, making sure we had a good view of the entire room. Neither of us slept that night. That was the last night we ever spent in the guest room.

The headless man is one of many experiences we had at our grandfather's house. To this day, I am not sure what or who the entity was. I just know we were one of many who had witnessed and experienced the headless man.

CHAPTER 5
Henry the Cat Man (1993)

AFTER BECOMING ACQUAINTED with some of the older folks who lived in the neighborhood, I met Ms. Betty, who told me several stories about old Oak Cliff. She told one about a black man who worked in the nearby train yard and had lost his life in an accident. Now, supposedly, the man haunted the area close to where my grandfather lived.

The story goes that the man was sadistic and cruel to animals, especially cats. He loved to trap them and tie them to the train tracks and let the train run over them. One day he tripped while chasing a feline along the tracks. He accidently lost his footing and banged his head on the rails, knocking himself out. The next train ran him over, cutting off his head and legs. They buried him next to the train tracks. Because of his cruel nature, he had no friends or family to claim him. I asked her if the story was true.

"Yes. His name was Henry and he was an angry man," she answered. When she was a child, growing up in Oak Cliff, her parents would warn her about Henry, the cat man. He would wander around the neighborhood with his stick, knocking over trashcans, looking for cats to kill. "He was a sick man," she explained.

Ms. Betty was well past her 80s when she told the story. She was a kid when her parents told *her* the legend. Her voice quivered as she recounted her parents' words, " 'Go to sleep Betty, and if you don't, the cat man will crawl out of his grave and climb up your window to look for his head.' Just listen for the train and you'll know the cat man is around." She added, "Now every time you hear the train coming in the middle of the night, that means the old, headless train conductor is crawling close to your house. You would also know because the cats warn you when he's around."

I am not sure if her story is true, but I know what Juan and I experienced at grandfather's house, and it was real. So, if you ever wake up in the middle of the night and hear a train in the distance, followed by a cat's meow, beware… Henry, the cat man, is close behind.

CHAPTER 6
One Bad Night (1993)
Part 1: Nightwalker

MY STORY BEGINS one night in October when the first cold wind blew in from the north. It had been raining for days now, increasing the wind chill to uncomfortable temperatures – unseasonably cool for Dallas. The leaves had begun to change their hue to a burnt orange. The moon was full that night and that was a bad omen, especially if I decided to visit Shelly. I was a nightwalker. 'Maybe I should cancel,' I thought. 'It's too bright to hide in the shadows,' as I tried to convince myself, pacing back and forth in the living room. It was dangerous, and with the full moon, the probability that something could go wrong was high.

Unable to burn up nervous energy, I went outside and sat on the porch steps, watching my legs twitch and dance in uncontrollable spasms. Drizzle covered the lawn, the drops sparkling under the streetlight, and amplifying the smell of dead leaves. I was anticipating Shelly's nightly call. 'She'll call me any minute now. I can feel it in my bones,' I hoped. I was standing guard on the phone because my brother had been known to tie it up for hours. If I needed privacy, the cord was long enough for me to pull it across the house and into the yard.

Time passed and I hadn't received her call. I went back inside feeling something was wrong. Shelly was like clockwork and never missed our nightly call. 'I'm in a bind now,' I thought. We had agreed no matter what, that we would see each other every first Thursday of the month, which meant I would see her tonight. Midnight and no call yet, as I sat in the darkness. I still hadn't received a confirmation. 'So, should I still go on my journey?' I asked myself. If I didn't, and she went out looking for me, she might be in danger. I couldn't live with myself if something happened to her. I decided to take a chance and make my trek.

I always loved the weather this time of the year – not too cold or hot, but not tonight. The temperature continued to drop as the rain stopped. 'It's a good sign,' I told myself as I gathered everything I needed for the trip.

I made the sign of the cross on my forehead, in hopes that God would look after me. Second thoughts danced in my head as I covered my mouth and nose with the black scarf my mother had given me for my birthday. My nightwalker outfit was not thick enough to keep the cold out, so I grabbed Juan's black hoody with pockets to keep my hands warm. The hoody was typical of what a street gang member would wear, and I hesitated to take it, but I was cold, and I had no choice, *and* I had to return it before he got home from his date.

Like Shakespearean characters, Shelly was my Juliet and I risked my life every time I went to see her. At the stroke of midnight, like clockwork, I traveled from my house and walked about three miles through local nature preserves, haunted creek beds, gang-infested streets, and police-patrolled shopping centers to see her. These excursions were dangerous and foolish, and in retrospect, I am surprised I didn't get killed. I went on this journey at least three times a week for about two years.

After a year, I became an expert nightwalker. I had learned to evade any obstacle that presented itself. It was life or death, so I took my journey seriously, making sure to map out the safest path and predict any danger before it happened. I memorized police patrol patterns and mapped out gang territories. Camouflage was a key part of my plan, so I dressed all in black, wearing a dark hood and matching scarf to cover my face. My nightwalker outfit would be frightening to look at if you'd happen to encounter me at night, especially with my favorite weapon at my side – and that was the point. I learned to stay in the darkness, always. Venturing out at night, in the 'hood, a person needed to be invisible to passing cars and people.

I carried what I considered my support supplies: cash for bus ride or call; St. Michael's prayer card, and an old, wooden rosary my grandmother gave me to ward off evil spirits and demons; a weapon. My weapon – what I called Morning Star – was a baseball bat wrapped in black electrical tape with nails hammered on the working end. I called it that because it reminded me of the weapon that a vampire hunter used in the Castlevania video game. If I got in trouble, my best option was to evade and escape. Using a weapon was my last choice, if it came down to a fight. I tied a rope around both ends so I could carry morning star on my shoulder, making it easier to transport. I needed to keep my hands free just in case I had to make a quick exit.

I'm truly surprised I wasn't mistaken for a burglar because of my outfit. Another reason I covered my face with a scarf was that I found that if I didn't, I would experience more paranormal activity than usual. Even worse, the dead would follow me home. The scarf acted sort of like a mask, the way fourteenth century Italian doctors wore the bird beak masks. Although they wore these facades to protect themselves from being infected by disease, some also say they wore masks so the dead wouldn't recognize them and follow them home. It's the same principle, except my scarf just covered my nose and mouth only. I needed to strike fear in anyone that I came across on my journey. If I did encounter another person, attire and accessories would usually scare them into running away from me, but this wasn't the case all the time.

One of my bigger threats wasn't paranormal but local gangs that claimed the neighborhoods. Every street had hoodlums associated with it, and I created my path to avoid those dangers. There were a few times we crossed paths, but I was too quick and would escape into the shadows. There's one thing about Latino gangs – they believe in superstitions – so most of them wouldn't follow me, thinking I was a ghost or some other type of supernatural evil.

Like it or not, I was making the trip tonight. I reached for my bat and headed out to Shelly's house. I had mapped out the safest route, so the only things I had to worry about were the police and the ghetto birds that patrolled the neighborhoods. Since it was so bright tonight, so I decided to take the nature preserve path, which meant I had to follow the train tracks into a spillway that I thought of as a dead man's creek.

One Bad Night (1993)
Part 2: Into the Darkness

THE STREETS WERE empty, which I expected. The rain had made the sidewalk muddy, so I opted to walk on the wet pavement. I reached the bridge next to the trailer park without anyone noticing me. The trailer park was adjacent to an old bridge built in the 1940's to segregate the white neighborhood from the poorer blacks. The bridge connected northern Oak Cliff from the southern area. I had made this journey many times and taking the bridge was dangerous because of the projects. Going into the projects at night was suicide. I needed to go underneath the bridge to avoid the gangs, so I made my way down a small trail, which I had used before. The path took me under the bridge and straight to the trailer park. But first, I had to jump a fence into a heavily treed section to access the area under the bridge.

As I made my way through the tall grass, I noticed someone walking in the darkness. I immediately felt a strange type of energy. The back of my head started to tingle. This energy left familiar. I recognized the presence of something evil. I quickly raised my morning star in case I needed to defend myself.

"He, he, he," came from the darkness. I heard a low giggle coming from behind the stone bridge pillar.

'There shouldn't be anyone here, certainly not at this hour,' I pondered, getting ready to run or fight. I stopped mid-stride, standing straighter with a deeper breath, to appear more dangerous than I was. I was hoping to scare the other person, while desperately looking for an escape – but nothing. There was no place to hide. My heart rate increased as I realized I had few options. It was either: run back and leap over the fence, or ignore the person walking towards me. I decided to stay and blend into the darkness, hearing the stress in the wood of my bat as I gripped it tighter. Nothing good ever traveled at night, so whoever it was, was not good.

Scrape, scrape, scrape, the sound of a foot dragged across the ground. A quiet giggle, like that of a child, pierced the night.

'What's a kid doing under a bridge?' I asked myself. My skin crawled when I noticed a small figure coming my way. It was a small child holding onto a weathered blanket, traveling slowly across the bottom of the bridge next to the tall grass. *Scrape, scrape, scrape*, still the only sound I could hear as it walked closer.

I lowered my bat as I took a good look at the child. An awful odor of decay and sulfurous brimstone filled my lungs. Quickly, I stepped back in horror as a small, mummy-like corpse continued toward me. Her head was drooped with missing clumps of blond hair. She wore a polka dot dress and one red shoe, dragging a bare foot behind her. *Scrape, scrape, scrape*, it slowly advanced in a trance-like manner.

Locking eyes on the child, who had just been in the ravine, it suddenly stopped. As it passed me, it turned its gross, decayed head and smiled. Or, at least what I think was a smile, because her face was a shell of grey eyes and leathery skin stretched over her skull. Her arm stretched out almost like she wanted to hold hands. Its decayed hand slowly reached out to me, and for a second I almost reached out to give it comfort. Coming to my senses for a second, I decided to grab my rosary instead. The ghoul quickly retracted its hand and kept walking.

Shaking my head, I suddenly began to gather my thoughts as I watched her disappear underneath the darkness of the bridge pillars. Sadness came over me because I knew she was a lost soul. But I couldn't help her and I wasn't sure if she even was a kid. Whatever it was, I had no time for it tonight. I took out my St. Michael's card and read the small passage on the back of the card. I didn't want the spirit to follow me home. I turned around one last time to make sure the child wasn't behind me. That's when I noticed two glowing eyes peering from the other side of the furthest pillar. I could also make out a huge smile. 'Just ignore it,' I said to myself, rereading the St. Michael's card, walking to the trailer park.

I finally made it to the trailer park gates next to the ravine. It wasn't an easy path to navigate because I had to cross a drug-infested trailer park full of dope fiends, child molesters, and other not so upstanding types. In the park, I passed an overweight Caucasian hooker with big hair sitting outside her trailer. I'd seen her before, actively hooking on Fort Worth Avenue. Her black pimp waited in an old, yellow Cutlass Supreme with Daytona wire rims that made the car run low to the ground. I knew she had to be in her early twenties, but her face looked aged from drug use. She was wearing a pink top and shorts that barely left anything to the imagination. The woman was smoking an unfiltered blunt; the smell of cheap marijuana filled my nostrils. We made eye contact for a second. She puckered her ruby red lips together making a kissing gesture and quickly walked into her mobile home.

Resuming my walk towards a set of defunct train tracks, I immediately turned around when I heard the high-pitched hooker's voice. She was talking to her old pimp. Small in stature, I could see his shaved head and bare belly sagging below his belt line. His weathered, ashy skin seemed to glow in the dark.

"He went that way. I think he was a Five-O – nothin' but trouble," as she pointed her long red nails in my direction. I quickly ducked underneath a nearby bush, tightened the grip on Morning Star, and all the while, kept my eyes locked on her pimp. Thankfully, he never saw me.

"Bitch, you crazy," he replied and quickly walked back into his smoked-filled trailer. I needed to move faster. I was drawing too much attention.

The air was heavy and the tracks seemed to float above the unkempt brush and abandoned cars. The old train tracks told a story of former Dallas when the north divided the south, its rusted tracks and overgrown ferns along its side. This was the fastest way to cover ground without being spotted. I finally made it past the train tracks and down to the nature preserve. Now I had to cross into the most dangerous zone of my route where I'd be past the point of no return, South Oak Cliff.

I lived in North Oak Cliff, known at the time as Little Mexico, because of the large number of Mexican families in the area. The south end was to be avoided because of the overly violent black gangs that owned the streets. If they spotted me, I'd be killed without question.

This gang-infested area just happened to be where my girlfriend lived, so I had no choice. All I had to do was walk four blocks out in the open to her house, or, walk the wilderness preserve, a safer route, but also haunted. The nature preserve and adjacent creek were used, mostly by gangs, for disposing of bodies of murdered victims. Bullet or ghost, the creek bed was a natural choice, but this time it was flooded. I had no option but to take door #2 through gang territory. All the while, I still couldn't shake the feeling that something was wrong. We didn't have cell phones at the time, so there was no way I could call Shelly and cancel. I didn't want her to try and meet me if I wasn't there. She could be raped or murdered if I didn't show up.

I had attuned my hearing as part of my nightcrawling skills. I could identify an auto before seeing it, thus aiding quick concealment. This time, I didn't realize I had been spotted. *Pop, pop, pop*! I heard three shots from a 9mm swish by my head. Before I could react, I heard a car speeding towards me. I noticed a young black man in a bright blue flannel shirt sitting by the passenger window pointing a gun in my direction.

'Oh shit,' I thought. My first instinct was to escape and evade. I went on autopilot, running in the direction of the nature preserve and dove head first into the woods, thick with pecan and oak trees, next to the creek. Luckily, the bullets whizzed by me. Panicked, I hadn't noticed the deep ravine because of the overgrown bushes. *Pop, pop, pop*! The air was shattered with bright, metal fireflies as I tumbled down to the bottom of the ravine. I heard a voice come from the street next to the entrance of the nature preserve where I had just been. *Pop, pop, pop*! Bullets continued to tear through the trees. The youth, not much older than me, blindly unloaded his 9mm in my direction. Silence fell upon the night.

He called out to his friends, "That nigga went this way." More headlights shown, meaning more members had joined the hunt.

I tumbled down the hill towards the creek and was dropping so rapidly that I couldn't control my fall. I felt branches and brush stabbing my body and scratching my face. Still hearing gunfire behind me, I smacked into a huge oak tree. The impact knocked the air out of my lungs and my vision faded. Shaking my head to reorient, I quickly moved behind the tree. After catching my breath, I followed a small path next to the creek to evade the gunfire. About the same time, headlights and the voices penetrated the woods. I looked around trying to find a hiding place because there was no way I could outrun my pursuers.

Out of nowhere, this old man appears behind some bushes like a jack-in-a-box, startling me. I figured he had heard the gunshots and hid behind the bushes, like me. Instinctively, I reached for my bat and held it in a striking position. He just stood there and pointed at an area next to the ravine. It was too dark to really take in the details, but he looked like an old *cholo*, or Mexican gangster.

He wore a flannel shirt over a wife beater and brown cut-offs. My heart jumped as I noticed his face – or lack thereof. He was missing half his head from a shotgun blast. His open mouth was frozen in a perpetual scream and his only eye was a white marble, hanging by a stalk in his head; it was looking in another direction. His skin looked like weathered boot leather but I could still see the tattoos on his arm as he pointed toward the creek. He gave me a 'What's up?' nod when we made eye contact. I couldn't shake the feeling that as hideous as he looked, he was familiar to me; I had seen this man before.

Trusting, I quickly made my way through the brush where he had pointed. There was a hidden area off the trail I hadn't noticed that would conceal my escape. I turned back to the *cholo*, but he had vanished. Getting into the water, the current was strong and near overflowing, because of the recent rain. After submerging the lower half my body in the cold water, I began to twitch and shiver uncontrollably. My legs became achy and stiff. It felt like hands were on my ankles trying to pull me into the creek. My heart pounded and my stomach clenched in unrelenting spasms. What made things worse? Ants chewing my legs, biting me as they trailed up my inner thighs to sting my arms. Wobbling, I grabbed a thorny branch to gain balance when I realized I was trapped.

I heard a voice from the trail I had just left. It was the street thug again. That crazy nut was at my front, the creek at my back. He was waving his gun wildly, in all directions, when the rest of the gang surrounded me. Headlights were illuminating the grounds, so my only thoughts were to stay motionless, blend into the darkness, and pray to God. Getting killed tonight was not part of my plan. The thug unloaded his gun near me until we heard the police sirens.

"Let's get the fuck out of here!" someone in the background shouted. Soon the ghetto bird arrived, its spot light searching the nature preserve in the opposite direction from where I was hiding. I finally crawled out of the creek once I was sure they were gone and shucked my pants to get those damned ants off my legs and arms. I waited for what seemed like an hour and then made my way back to the street.

A sense of relief came over me. I was thankful to the person, or whatever it was, that told me where to hide. He must have been another lost soul from the dead man's creek. This time, I stayed as silent as possible, hiding behind every car I could find on my way to see Shelly. Death would not come between Shelly and me.

One Bad Night (1993)
Part 3: The Promised Land

I FINALLY MADE it to Shelly's house about an hour late. I knew from the beginning that something was very wrong tonight, but I didn't care anymore. I placed my bat next to the trashcan in her alley. Excited to see her, I quickly jumped over her fence with one stride and found her asleep by her bedroom window. I'd been through hell and the sight of her warmed my heart. "Pssst, pssst, pssst," I quietly called out to her. A beautiful face appeared from the darkness as I could see her waking smile. Her eyes lit up as she saw me; she waved back. She disappeared into the darkness to make her way to the back door. The door slowly opened.

"Hey, about time. I heard gunshots. You okay?" she said, speaking softly, and kissed me. Without saying a word, I reached out and gently caressed her beautiful face, pulling her to me for another long, passionate kiss.

"Come on, let's go to my room," as she said, smiling. She grasped my hand tightly so I wouldn't get lost in the darkness. As she turned, I slowly followed her along the carpeted passage. A different fear came over me as she pushed me against the wall, placing her hand on my neck. We had to be quiet since her parents were asleep.

"Why didn't you call me? I was worried," I quietly asked.

"Sh-h-h, be quiet," she said, giving me a devilish smile. I think the excitement of getting caught aroused her, but scared me. I could feel her hips tilted against mine as her breasts pressed against my chest. I knew it was dangerous to sneak into her room, but the exhilaration drove us to take that chance. I could get beat up or shot by her family, but I didn't care. They hated everything about me, and I didn't blame them. According to them, I was just a street thug, but I loved her, and that's what she loved about me. My time with her was magical, so if I died in her arms tonight, it would be a heavenly way to die. I know it sounds crazy, but a love like ours was insane and deadly. That's why I was willing to walk the night.

She was wearing her typical attire, fitted soccer shorts and a small red tank top that highlighted her breasts. She had her red glasses on, giving her the sexy librarian look. I loved the way she pinned up her hair in a bun so it wouldn't get in the way. My teenage mind exploded as she kissed my neck. I broke out in goosebumps, as I closed my eyes.

"This is where I belong, with you in my arms," as I said, as I smiled back. I picked her up by her hips, and she wrapped her legs around me; she felt so warm. She resumed kissing my neck as she started to remove my shirt.

"I was so worried about you," murmuring, as she placed her head on my chest.

"You won't lose me," I spoke softly into her ear. Even though she had lit several candles in her room, they provided little visibility. I didn't need it. She pulled me closer to give me a long soft kiss.

'How lucky can a man be,' I thought. I could taste her lipstick, cherry-flavored. I loved the way she smelled, unlike me. I knew I smelled like creek water. She clasped me to her, feeling my heartbeat, then gave me a worried expression. I took a deep breath and embraced her tighter in relief. She asked me, "What happened? Are you all right?" She sensed I wasn't going to tell her, and I couldn't tell her.

"I'm here, and that's all that matters now," I responded. If she knew what had happened to me she wouldn't let me see her again. Just being with her was all I wanted.

Fatigue had started to set in, and I could barely keep my eyes open. Shelly sat me on her bed and slowly undressed in front of me. I tried to burn her image onto my brain because I didn't want to forget this moment. The adrenaline had dwindled, and now I could feel the bruising, insect bites, and scratches of the night. Shelly stretched out to hold me, whispering in my ear "You're so cold." Shelly saw my fresh wounds from the trip over and asked me, "Am I worth it?"

I answered quickly, "Yes, without question." I hissed as she slowly ran her hand across the bruise on my chest.

"I want to take your breath away and the ache I know you have. I want to please you in every single way and excite your senses. I missed you, and I love you forever." I smiled back and hugged her, both of us passionately embraced in the darkness. What we had was so natural. I thought I knew now how Romeo felt, and I too, would die for love.

It seemed like hours had passed, as we both lie on her bed looking up at the popcorn ceiling. The echo of thunder in the distance, and the constant sound of police sirens, we both realized I still had to make the journey home. Worried about me, she asked me to stay over, but that was a crazy pipe dream. I heard her father snoring from the other side of the wall. It was time for me to go. Her parents would be up any minute. Disappointed I had lost so much time, I didn't stay as long as I wanted too. We heard her father get up and turn on his light.

"I heard something, let me check on Shelly," her father spoke, from the other side of the wall. Suddenly we heard footsteps coming down the hall toward her room. Her dad was on his way.

"Oh shit! My dad heard us!" she said, panicking as she reached for her clothes and gave me mine. "Hurry, put your stuff on, quick," she whispered in a frantic tone. We both were fearful of making a sound. This was the first time I'd ever seen Shelly afraid. She quickly put her hand over my mouth. "Stay still," she implored, as the reality of the situation sunk in.

"How did I find myself in this circumstance again?" I wondered, trapped, but this time in her room. She murmured, "Hide under the bed, quick!" Shelly had a big queen size, so it was easy to hide under the frame. The sound of heavy footsteps shuffling in the hall got closer. My heart sank into my stomach as the steps stopped in front of her door. The doorknob gradually turned halfway, *creeeeeak*, the door slowly opened. Once more, my life flashed before my eyes because this man would shoot me on sight. We both waited for him to walk in but he never did. At the last minute, he stopped and closed the door. He instead, walked past her door toward the bathroom. A little while later we heard the sound of the toilet flushing and the shuffling back to his bedroom. Time seemed to slow while we waited to hear her father snore once more. It was past time for me to leave. She walked me to the back door. I noticed a shotgun next to the back door – it wasn't there before.

'Maybe he did hear us and this was a warning,' I thought. I had to be smarter next time. My days of sneaking into her room could be over.

"Be careful, and call me when you get home," Shelly whispered.

I agreed and gave her one last kiss and whispered, "See you soon." She looked worried as I made my way into the alley again. I couldn't take any more surprises. I just wanted to go home.

One Bad Night (1993)
Part 4: The Beast of Oak Cliff

My Morning Star was still in the same spot I left it, and I was beyond tired. It was late and I had a long journey in front of me. The night had gotten colder and I could feel the freezing breeze hit my face like a whip. On impulse, I turned back toward her house one last time, but she had already gone inside. I slowly put on my hoody, lifting one tired arm at a time. The hoody had green skid marks and dry leaf crumbs from my fall. I didn't care – it was my brother's hoody. My entire body hurt and fatigue dulled my senses enough that I could hardly keep my eyes open. My mind didn't care anymore. I just trudged.

The moon was still visible and the shadows it created played tricks on me. The path I decided to take home was the trail that guided me through the business district of Oak Cliff. I figured there would be enough cops in the area to keep the gang members away, so it was the safest way home. It was about four in the morning now and I was running late because school would start in a few hours. Besides being tired and bruised, I felt better. All the trouble I had gone through was worth it in the end, because, after all, I got to see Shelly. Now I had to make it back before my parents woke up.

After walking through dark alleys and neighborhoods, I made it back to the same street where I was almost murdered, but this time, everyone was gone. I walked down Madison Avenue, bypassing the trailer park and the projects, toward Jefferson Street, without drawing attention. Besides, the only people up this hour were the cops and crazies, like me. It was a longer walk, but I decided I didn't want to take a chance.

'So far so good,' I thought, as I looked for police patrols on Jefferson. "No barking from the dog, no hog, everything was good," the lyrics of an Ice Cube song played in my head. It was all clear. 'Maybe my luck has changed for the better,' I thought.

Across the street was the corner drug store, which was the halfway point of my journey. Once I crossed the street, I was in my neighborhood and relatively safe. My clothes were still soaked and the cold wind was really giving me chills. I had also lost a new black scarf when I tumbled down the ravine, so my face felt like it was freezing. The drug store had an alley that would block the wind and big enough to hide in, in case I had to escape the police.

All of a sudden, the unmistakable odor of a wet dog caught my attention, followed by a horrendous overpowering stench of urine and decay. I almost gagged. 'What the hell?' I thought, covering my mouth from the awful odor.

Out of nowhere, I heard a loud snarl that rattled my bones and stopped me in my tracks. It seemed as though it was coming from everywhere and followed by a deep roar that only a massive beast could make; I froze. The growl stopped abruptly and I quickly turned, looking for the origin of the snarl.

I raised my bat, creeping along, expecting to see a big dog. The noise was coming from behind some dumpsters. All my survival instants told me to walk away. I didn't want to come across whatever made that noise. Foolishly though, I had to know.

The loud growling resumed. Again, I couldn't move. I didn't know if it was fear or some unknown force had paralyzed me. The growling stopped for a second and finally, I could move again. Not wasting another second, I raised the bat over my head. Then I saw what shouldn't exist.

An enormous beast was digging in a dumpster. I realized the dumpster had to be at least eight feet tall – translation – this creature had to be at *least* nine feet tall. I couldn't view its whole body, but what I could see was two hairy elbows from the top of the trash container. Adrenaline surging, I was coiled to strike, as I crept closer. I noticed two massive, muscular legs covered in dark fur, attached to human-shaped buttocks with a hairy, wolf-like tail at the base of its black-furred spine. Its tail wagged at a furious pace, as if content with whatever it found in the trash. The leg muscles powerfully flexed as it moved effortlessly around and inside the dumpster on large canine paws.

'How big is this brute? Half its body is stretched inside this dumpster and the dumpster is moving,' I wondered incredulously. The creature suddenly stopped and took two loud snorts, tested the air, and roared as it sniffed again. It had caught my scent; I stepped back. I heard it growl again, but this time I wasn't paralyzed. I slowly backed away making sure not to take my eyes off this werewolf. I mean, there was no other word to describe it – a werewolf.

All of a sudden, it was raised up out of the dumpster and sprang towards me. I turned and ran as fast as I could. Absolute terror came over me as adrenaline rocketed through my bloodstream. I knew if I ran in a straight line this animal would quickly have me for lunch because there was no way I could outrun it. I zigzagged and lost sight of it, but still glimpsed behind me just to make sure it was gone – it was. As I ran for my life, I sensed I was being stalked.

'Hell no! Not today,' I told myself, 'I did not survive tonight just to get mauled.' Over the hill was Elsbeth, the street I lived on. Just a few blocks more… I decided to take a shortcut through my neighbors' backyards. I wasn't going to make it. I felt it almost on me. I jumped a fence into a garden, ran, and jumped a chain link fence into another yard.

By this time, I could hear all the dogs in the neighborhood barking and howling. I ran like a mad man. I had made it to the last backyard next to the street by my old elementary school. Relief came over me as I could see my house from there. Sweat poured down my back and forehead. My hands clenched as I looked toward the last make or break hurdle – a huge wooden fence. It was eight feet tall, unlike the shorter chain link fences. I ran faster, betting my life I could leap the tall wall. Unfortunately, I was so exhausted I didn't clear it entirely. I lost my footing and tumbled down headfirst. Juan's hoody got caught on a fence plank, causing my face to take the brunt of the impact. All I could see now were stars, my head dizzy from the blow. My arm was pinned under my body.

A horrible odor came from the other side of the fence and I heard the loud growl; I froze. The beast was on the other side licking the wood plank, like it was doing a taste test where I had just touched.

Sniff, sniff, as the creature raised its nose to the air. That's when I heard a truck coming down the street. I quickly tore the sleeve on the hoody to free myself and ran in front of the vehicle's path. Hoping to grab the driver's attention, I waved my arms and heard the honking of the truck horn. The driver swerved to avoid me.

'This is it,' I thought as my life flashed before me. I closed my eyes waiting for the impact but it never came. The truck kept going, even as I tried to get him to pull over.

A sense of relief came over me since my home was three doors down. My elbow was cut deep enough to draw blood. I didn't care. Not wasting any more time, I quickly ran keeping a look out for the beast. Determination and willpower to survive kept me from complete exhaustion. I finally made it to my front lawn.

'Home, sweet, home. I made it without getting killed,' I thought. Feeling indestructible and brave, I decided to turn around for a second. 'What the hell was it?' I asked myself. I was determined to see the monster, but nothing. I looked down the street and didn't see anything. My father's truck was gone, that meant I was too late and would get busted when he came home from work. There was still time before my mother woke up, so I raced to the back door.

Halfway there, I heard a loud growl from behind me. "Shit!" as I ran through the back door of my house. Luckily, it was still unlocked. I tumbled forward after slamming the door behind me. The creature was outside the back door. It sniffed the air around the threshold where I had just crossed. 'How could I have missed something so massive?' I asked myself. It was almost like it just appeared behind me. I had barely escaped this animal. *Sniff, sniff,* as it continued to sniff at the bottom of the door. Its black tongue slowly and methodically licked every inch of the underside of the door, making whimpering sounds, like a dog in heat.

'Was it detecting Shelly's scent on me?' I thought as I sniffed my shirt, as I indeed had her scent all over me. The creature seemed to be in heat, as it licked and moaned at the door. 'It had to be a big black dog,' I told myself. What other explanation was there?

Everyone was asleep, so I still had time to make it to my bed. The sun was coming up as I watched the animal disappear into the backyard. I had had enough of the werewolf creature and ran into my room. A horrifying feeling came over me when I realized this creature could have killed me at any point. 'It let me get away, almost like it wanted to know where I lived. It showed intelligence and cunning, scaring me like a rabbit and making me run home. Is that what it wanted?' I pondered. The thought of the beast lurking scared me. 'Does it have another plan for me?' I couldn't get its growl out of my head. Luckily, since my father was already gone, I sat in my room thinking about what had just happened.

The sun was coming up, and I felt safe – for now. I quickly fell asleep. I spent too much energy running from gang bangers and the werewolf creature. It was a school night, so even though I only got an hour of sleep, I had nightmares of wolf-like monsters.

I woke up to the smell of bacon. My mother walked in and shot me with a water gun. I reluctantly got up and got dressed to go to high school. I looked like death himself since I was running on zero sleep.

My brother rushed into the kitchen, mad as hell, saying, "An animal chewed my bumper." We all ran outside, and sure enough, Juan's bumper and hood had huge bite marks. It wasn't a bad dream after all. The beast was real and this was proof. My brother walks out of his room with his hoody, asking, "What the fuck happened to my hoody?"

I answered, "Man you have really bad luck. First your car, now your hoody… that sucks dude. Maybe Dad wore it to work," I offered, quickly sitting down to have breakfast.

During class, thoughts of the Oak Cliff beast raced through my head, as I tried to stay awake. I believe God created all creatures on this planet, except for that thing. He did *not* have a hand in this… had to be the devil's work. I wasn't the only person to experience the beast that Fall. Unbeknownst to me, someone else on my street encountered that creature, as well.

One Bad Night (1993)
Part 5: Miguel's Story

I BARELY MADE it through class trying to stay awake. Normally, I would come home from Shelly's at a reasonable hour, but after this hellacious night, I was lucky to be alive. Thoughts of the man-wolf-monster raced in my head and kept me awake. Sleep deprivation would not stop me from finding out what I encountered last night and the best spot to research this was the school library. Usually, I wouldn't be caught dead in that place, but today was different. I had to know more.

In the ghetto, the library is the safest place to be during school and I was by myself throughout my lunch period. After hours of reading old newspapers and articles, the only encounter of such creature was in El Paso in 1845, at the Devil's River near Del Rio, in southwest Texas. A boy who had lived in San Felipe Springs, reported seeing several enormous wolves and a creature having long hair covering its body. Sounded exactly like what I had witnessed. I'd heard of Bigfoot before and this wasn't Bigfoot. I had also read about the Dogman, but that was too hard for even me to believe.

Exhausted, I went home and got some sleep. After sleeping for several hours, I decided to retrace my steps. The evening was quiet, so I felt safe to stroll around my block, at least until night came. Near the back of the school next to the playground, I noticed a thin man, covered in tats, sitting by himself on the sidewalk curb. As I got closer, I realized it was my neighbor, Miguel. We nodded to each other, and I sat with him while he finished a joint.

We lived on the same block but his house was on a corner lot. It had that rundown appearance like a dope house and was unfortunately, the nicest house on the block. Miguel was about five years older than me and a hardcore gang member; the type you avoided making eye contact with in a dark alley. I enjoyed talking to Miguel about gang life and his beliefs, but what I liked the most was the fact that he had some pretty hot sisters. Miguel had a little brother, Angel, who liked hanging out with me. His family wasn't originally from Dallas but from southern Texas. Miguel had gotten in trouble, which forced his family to move to Oak Cliff. Everyone on my street knew and respected him. He was a typical Latino gang member, wearing a black, extra-large shirt and gray Dickies cut-offs.

"What's up, little homie?" he inquired, reaching out for a handshake. Miguel always seems to be smiling, regardless of what was going on. "Angel is with my dad, in case you're looking for him," he explained.

"I'm cool. What's up?" I had to tell someone what I saw last night. "Have you ever seen anything strange around here?" I asked, expecting to get clowned. Before I could say anything, he told me something strange.

"Remember last week when I got attacked by a homeless person?"

"Yes," I responded. Miguel was a heavy drug user, so at the time, I didn't believe his crazy story. That day stuck with me because his dad had come by looking for Angel. Miguel went on to explain what happened that night. His father was upset because Miguel had gotten beat up in the alley behind the Polar Bear Ice Cream shop next to the old Lake Cliff Park. I thought another gang banger had beaten him, but that wasn't the case. He said that he had gone to the 7-11 near the park with a friend. They went around midnight to buy snacks. On his way back, Miguel took a shortcut through the small alley behind the ice cream shop. That's when he noticed a man digging through the shop's dumpster.

"Look at this freak, *vato*," his friend called out to Miguel.

"Where you from, homeboy?" Miguel asked the stranger. The homeless person just ignored them and kept eating the trash from inside the dumpster. Miguel didn't like being ignored. He quickly grabbed a metal pipe from the alley, as he and his friend slowly walked past the trash digger. They heard a low growl, the type you hear when you try to take food from a hungry stray. At the time, they didn't find the growl strange, but what freaked them out was the fact the man was gargantuan and appeared to be wearing a fur coat.

"Let's go. Fuck that *puto*," Miguel told his friend, as they strolled past the strange man. A deeper growl erupted from the creature as they got closer. There is a point when one stops being a thug and reverts to being a child – they had reached this point. The friend grabbed Miguel's shirt in fear. Miguel still had the iron pole at his side. Confident they were safe, they made their way past the massive man. The instant Miguel turned, the behemoth grabbed and picked his friend with one hand, then slammed him to the ground. Miguel stepped back as he realized the man wasn't a man, but a beast. It started to maul his friend using massive claws and teeth as it ripped into his back. Luckily, his friend wore a heavy work jacket that blocked most of the damage.

"Help! Help me!" his friend screamed in terror. Miguel charged and started to beat what he thought was a man, on the head, with the pipe – enough for the thing to let go.

"I hit that fucker as hard as I could, but it didn't seem to feel anything. Then it turned around and looked at me," Miguel explained. With a straight and serious face, he said, "It stood up, like a man, and looked me in the eye with such hatred that it burned my soul. It scared the shit out of me and, for real, I almost shit my pants." I noticed his hands were shaking. By the sound of his voice, I was lucky the beast didn't attack me.

"The fucking thing then got down on all fours and it growled at me like an angry dog. Before it could attack again, I reached down and grabbed my homeboy. He was bleeding from his back and arms from trying to keep his face from getting shredded. It was trying for his neck. Out of nowhere, I go flying, landing couple of yards from my homie. It elbowed me so hard it knocked my Converse off my feet with one *chingaso*, as it made a run for the park. Next thing I know, my homeboy was dragging me by one arm down the street. It sounds crazy, right? But that fucker was the devil, *el diablo*, homie." Miguel said he ran home to his parents when he noticed blood seeping from his head.

"Did you see where it went?" I asked. He could tell I believe him. Any other circumstance, I would have said "Bullshit," but I saw the same creature last night.

"The fucker ran the opposite way toward the park," he explained.

"My *jefe* wasn't playing when he went looking for the goat man in his truck," explained Miguel. As proof, he showed me his stitches on the back of his head. Miguel's father was an old school lowrider from the South Texas Valley area and had spent time in prison. After this happened, his father took it upon himself to hunt the creature every night. He spent weeks looking for the attacker, driving slowly up and down the park area in his old Ford truck at night, but he never found it. The next day Angel and Miguel had a strict curfew.

I am sure Angel also told me the story, and at the time I thought it was crazy, but guess what? Maybe we saw the same thing. I asked Miguel to describe the monster. I was dying to know since I never got the chance to get a closer look. All he said was that it looked like it had a person's body and a dog's head. The long face had pointy, cropped ears like a dog. It was on all fours like a dog, then stood up like a person and just looked at them, before running away. Miguel called it the goat man, because its black hair it reminded him of a goat, but with the face of a dog and body of a man. I wouldn't have believed him, had I not seen the creature for myself. We weren't the only people to see this beast that year.

To this day, I have no clue what it was, nor do I want to see at it again. I do believe the creature came from the Trinity River Basin. It may have been following prey. Who knows? Maybe it was a wolf, a demon, or an unknown animal. All I know is that it was huge and it smelled like death itself. I am sure it didn't want me; it was tracking my girlfriend's scent. I don't even want to imagine its intentions. So be careful if you decide to take a walk in a nature preserve at night. You never know what lurks in the darkness. There are worse things out there than ghosts.

CHAPTER 7
It's Under the Bed (1993)
Part 1: The House Guest

A S A TEENAGER, I had many acquaintances but there were only a
few people I considered more haunted me. Frank lived on
a corner lot on Alabama in south Dallas, which was located
adjacent to a park. South Dallas, at the time, was a high crime area filled
with vacant lots and drug houses. It was mainly known as a low-income
black neighborhood with a mix of Latinos; therefore, it wasn't a place
where you wanted to be at night. He was my girlfriend's neighbor. Yes,
Shelly, the girl I sneaked around with at night. The house itself looked
like it was straight out of the nineteen-forties with old art deco design
and original color scheme of blue and white. Thick willow trees draped
across the roof like a veil for a wedding dress, giving the house have a
fairytale look, like it was part of an enchanted forest.

Frank was short. Everyone knows someone like Frank. You know,
the kid that never quite fit in with the crowd. He had oily, limp black
hair that covered his eyes. What made it worse? He always wore the
same clothes and he seemed always to be sweating, for no reason. Like
a puppy, he would follow around any person giving him attention.
I guess I blame myself, being a good guy, so I didn't stop him. I was
popular in high school, so it bothered me. I know it sounds terrible,

but to tell you the truth, I didn't even notice him at school, except for the occasional *what up?* nod.

Frank was a good kid in every sense of the word, or at least better than me. He attended church. He also had straight A's and perfect attendance, unlike me. I was struggling at school, and I figured maybe he could help me with my studies one day. Once I got to know him, I realized he was okay, in a nerdy kind of way.

Frank's younger sister, Mary, just happened to be Shelly's best friend, so it was fate for us to become friends. We didn't have much in common, except that we both could see ghosts. I wasn't aware of this fact until much later.

One day during school, he awkwardly asked me to spend the night. I didn't want to do a sleepover because I wasn't that cool with him. In the end, I decided to go ahead and spend the night. Of course, I had an ulterior motive for my decision.

I secretly had agreed to stay the night to see my girlfriend, Shelly. Sneaking into her house was getting dangerous, and this was a perfect solution for our circumstances. After all, her father had given us a warning by placing the shotgun next to the door. We both decided we would sneak out and rendezvous at Frank's family backyard. They had a guesthouse, which was conveniently unoccupied at the time.

According to plan, Shelly would sneak out of her home to see Mary, but in reality, she would hang out with me. I called my parents and they agreed to let me stay the night. I quickly informed Shelly that our plan was in motion and we set a time to meet. I hadn't seen her in a week, so we were impatient.

I never had the pleasure of meeting Mary before, so this first time we met it was a complete surprise to discover Frank and Mary were related. Shelly never actually mentioned Mary before, but Mary certainly knew about me. Frank wasn't the only family member at my high school. It so happened their cousin Becky attended Sunset High. She considered me a flirt and had nothing good to say about me. According to her, all I did was talk to girls all day, skip school, and cause trouble. I didn't agree, well, except for the skipping school part. So Mary made sure I knew she had her eye on me.

Mary was tall and slender with perfectly carved shoulders, long legs, and gorgeous long brown hair and eyes; I thought she was beautiful. She was the same age as Shelly... and score! If it didn't work out with Shelly, I would be all over her. What can I say? I was a hormone-driven teen. She was also fiercely protective of her brother and Shelly. The girls attended the same private school and quickly became best friends. Mary was picky about who she dated and didn't like to associate with what she considered hoodlums, so she wasn't happy that I was dating her best friend.

Like Frank, his parents were very religious and friendly. After they welcomed me, I scoped out the house to familiarize myself with the distance between his room and the back door. The intense smell of cooked chilies permeated the entire house. I noticed all kinds of figurines, holy crosses, and Catholic saints though out the living room. Religious artifacts weren't uncommon for a Mexican home, so I didn't pay those much mind. His house had an unusually large number of horse flies, mostly gathered in windows and the kitchen. I was disgusted; they should get them exterminated.

Preoccupied with thoughts of Shelly, I sat down for dinner and started to eat as fast as I could. I was so hungry shoveling in food that I failed to notice no one else was eating. When I finally looked up, they began to pray and give thanks. Mary quickly realized I wasn't there to hang out with her brother. Angry, she gave me the stink-eye from across the table.

'Oops,' I thought. Man, did I feel stupid for not following their lead. Praying wasn't something my family did during meals. I apologized for my lack of manners and joined them in prayer. Mary tried to hide her laughing under a fake smile while I turned red. After an awkward dinner, we sat around and discussed current political topics. His parents suggested Frank show me around. Mary intervened quickly and asked me a couple of questions about Shelly. Of course, I played dumb and introduced myself.

"I know who you are," she snipped. "You're a flirt," she then chided. Noticing I wasn't going to play her game of volley to defend myself, she got upset and huffed off to her room.

"Bye, Mary," I called out to her. She turned around and gave me her middle finger. "Maybe later," I replied, as she slammed her bedroom door.

"Forget her," Frank said, "She's always mad at something, plus, I think she likes you." He also turned around to walk into his room. Frank began showing me his video games and comic book collection. When he noticed I wasn't paying attention he suggested we should watch television.

'Just put up with him until tonight,' I told myself. I listened to him talk about church while looking out his window at Shelly's house. 'What's she doing? Is she thinking about me?' I wondered, reviewing the plan in my head. I intended to sleep on the living room couch so I could make a quiet escape through the back door. 'What I do for love…' justified everything.

I stayed quiet while Frank droned on. Hours passed while waiting for the agreed rendezvous time. His mother walked into the room before going to bed and asked us not to stay up too late. I asked Frank if I could sleep on the living room couch. He quickly responded by asking me if I'd rather bunk in his room. I finally confessed my plan to see Shelly and asked him if he was going to snitch on me. He laughed, saying he was already knew because the glare Mary had given me. "Look, Oscar, if I had a girlfriend like Shelly, I would have done the same thing," as we both laughed. I felt that a huge weight had been lifted off my shoulders.

"Here's the plan, Frank, I want to spend time with Shelly. When I get back, I'll crash on the floor in your room," I responded.

"Please come back soon. I need your help," he whispered. He looked like a frightened child.

"What's wrong? Is something the matter?" I was getting curious. Maybe Frank had an ulterior motive.

"I know you can see them, too," he said.

"See who? What?" I wondered aloud.

"The dead," he answered back. I was shocked because I couldn't believe he knew. How could he have known? It's not like I broadcast that I see ghosts. Only a few people from my inner circle knew of my gift, and Frank wasn't part of that group.

I guess I kinda already knew he could, too. It's a type of energy I can feel, but it wasn't my place to call him out on it. I didn't want to seem creepy and strange. Just imagine if someone told you your house had a ghost. What would you think? The few people who knew about my secret already thought I was strange. I sat down on his couch wondering how to help him. So many questions ran through my head, so I started with the obvious and most important one.

"How can I help you?" I asked.

Frank asked me, stone cold expression, "Has something ever attacked you?" I paused for a second as images of the pig man came back to me. 'It can't be *that* bad,' I thought.

I answered, "Yes. Yes there has," I told him about the pig man and how he had viciously attacked me for many years. Curious, he began asking questions. I said, "Let's talk about you," because the time to meet Shelly was soon approaching. "Does it come at night?"

"Yes, it does," he replied, almost crying.

"Does it or he hurt you?" I expected some hesitation because it's such a personal question, but Frank responded immediately by lifting his shirt.

That's when I saw fresh scars on his chest and back. It was like some animal had raked its claws across his body, gouging deep furrows in the skin. The sight of this turned my stomach. 'What could have done this?' I wondered? Experiencing physical communication with the dead, like *this*, was something I had never seen before. On his chest was a bloody outline spelling out *I hate you* and on his back, the word *Die*.

"Holy shit!" I yelled, quickly lowering my voice again. I didn't want to wake up Frank's parents in the other room. It was the top of the hour and Shelly would soon be walking into the backyard. "Yes, I can help you, but let me go see my girlfriend first. I'll be back soon. Just wait for me in the living room, but whatever you do, *don't* fall asleep." He agreed, nodding his head. 'What can I do? This is so way out of my league,' I thought. I quickly freshened up and promised him I'd return, as he walked me to the back door.

"I'll leave the door unlocked, so just walk in," he suggested.

"Thanks, I will be back soon," I replied. He smiled and walked back into the living room.

My heart fluttered as I caught Shelly's beautiful smile. She was already waiting for me next to the guesthouse. "Come on. Let's go in before someone sees us," she waved her hand, opening the door. Unbeknownst to me, Mary had already unlocked the door for Shelly.

I turned around one last time, looking back at Frank's house. That's when I noticed someone looking through his window. Maybe it's him checking on me – I wished. I got a bad feeling and I knew he wasn't kidding. "Maybe I'm sensing *mal* from the park," I thought.

Their cozy guesthouse consisted of one bedroom, a living room, and a small kitchen. Shelly gave me a long kiss and murmured, "I missed you, babe." She took my hand and set me on the loveseat. Perched on my lap, her skin was cool and I could feel the goosebumps over her smoothly shaved legs. She had her usual scent of perfume and mix of lotion, and wearing soccer shorts and black tank. I felt happy to see her, but also kinda weird.

The last time we saw each other, we almost got caught by her father. Tonight felt awkward, off. 'Why does this feel strained?' I thought she might be cheating on me. She wasn't calling every night like she used to do.

'Maybe it's just teenage paranoia,' the angst at the thought of her with another man gripped me. "Don't trust a big booty and a smile," were the lyrics of a Bell Biv Devoe song that came to mind. And all the while, she's looking at me with her devilish smile. The paranoia of her parents discovering her absence to meet a boy in the middle of the night, were, well, too real.

Paranoia cast aside, I was a fool and I didn't care. All I wanted was Shelly. I know what she wanted and I wanted it too. This may sound so cliché but my love for her wasn't just physical. I felt she was my soulmate and I would gladly give her the world.

I gently picked her up like it was our wedding night and carried her to the bedroom. "Surprise," she whispered into my ear. Shelly had taken the time to light white candles all over the room. Like Shakespeare's tragedy, we both knew this was a forbidden romance. But I wouldn't have wanted it any other way. She would eventually move on and find someone else her parents liked. I loved her regardless, so I cherished anytime I got to spend with her.

I smiled back, lying down in the dimly lit room. Shelly straddled me and put her hands on my throat. "I will kill you if you cheat on me," she playfully suggested. Strange, that's exactly what I had been thinking about her.

"Let's run away together," she whispered. "I love you with all my heart. You know that, right?" as she stopped to look at me. The way she said it, was almost like she was saying goodbye. I answered aloud because I knew she expected me to reply.

"You're my life, my reason for being. I would die for you. And if I died tonight, it would be worth it, because I got to love you one last time." She smiled, as if satisfied with my answer, and curled next to me like a cat seeking warmth.

"What are we doing?" she asked. "It's not fair for you to risk your life to see me. What if something happened to you? I wouldn't be able to live without you," she said, putting her head on my chest. I didn't answer because I knew I couldn't promise her I would be safe.

We enjoyed each other's company as the time quickly passed. I had to leave. She gave me one last kiss after I walked her to the edge of the fence. I heard crickets chirping as the autumn breeze twirled her hair. I took one more look at her. I knew this would be one of the last times I would see her.

Soon after that night, she met someone else at her school and our relationship was over. There's more to our story, but that's for another time. I plan to write a separate book about my life with Shelly. I watched her go back to her house as she waved goodbye to me. I made my way back to Frank's house. Sneaking into houses was my specialty, after all, so I crept through the kitchen into the living room.

It's under the Bed (1993)
Part 2: Battle with a Demon

FRANK WAS STILL watching television in the living room when I returned.

"I am ready to help you, so let's do this," I whispered, so as not to wake his parents. He nodded as we tiptoed to his room. "I have a plan," I explained. "Just go to sleep, Frank," as I assured him I would take care of things, "And don't worry."

I had confidence – maybe because I had just been with Shelly. I promised him that in the morning everything would be all right. Deep inside, I was scared shitless. I really had no clue what I was doing. He quickly fell asleep while I stretched out on his bedroom floor with an old bed sheet and one of his pillows. Shelly's scent was still on me, which brought me some comfort. All I wanted to do was go home, but I had promised Frank, so I would at least try. If things got bad, I could always walk home.

I'd never tried to call a spirit before. Usually, the dead come to me, so I really didn't know if I could summon one. I got on my knees and started to pray. When I mean pray, I mean I recited every prayer I could think of, in the hope of aiding me some way. It was about 2 a.m. and I could not keep my eyes open. As I drifted to sleep in the darkness, the thought of Shelly's body gave me a warm, content feeling. I could still taste her lipstick and felt my lips curve into a smile, as I fell into a deep slumber.

In the middle of a dream, a tapping sound awakened me. I awoke to a thick fog that had settled in the room, as I rubbed my eyes to clear my own fog and focus on the tapping. My Scooby sense tingled because I felt a dark presence near me. I knew something was in the room with us. Frank seemed to be having a nightmare as he tossed and turned in his bed. The tapping sound made me turn my head toward the window. *Tap, tap, tap.* The type of sound someone would make to get your attention. Maybe it was Shelly at the window. I looked outside, but nothing. It was just an ever-consuming darkness. The entity was somewhere in the room, and, it knew I was here. It was time and I was prepared to do battle to expel it back to hell.

I whispered into the darkness, "I know you're here." I spoke softly into the corner of the room, "Please leave him alone, in God's name. You have no power here." In my experience, evil things like to hide in corners. Again, there was no response. 'Maybe there is nothing here after all,' I thought. I lie back down and looked up at the ceiling. "I am not scared of you," I whispered aloud, so as not to wake anyone in the house, but nothing. Another hour passed and it was now three in the morning. Still, I quickly fell into a deep sleep again.

The sound of tapping woke me up one more time. I opened my eyes and slowly turned my head toward the noise. I never get used to my fear of the dead, no matter how many times I've seen them. The sound was coming from all directions now. I focused my thoughts and tried to pinpoint the origin of the sound. I raised up to look outside the window. I saw the night sky but nothing out of the ordinary, just a couple of clouds around the tree line near the park.

Tap, tap, tap. The sounds repeated, but this time, faster and more deliberate. It wasn't coming from the window but from under Frank's bed. As I turned my head, I noticed a gray object run under the bed. I turned to get a better look but an oversized comforter almost reached the floor, so I couldn't really see the thing. I heard the tapping again and it seemed that something truly evil was playing the hot and cold game with me. The closer I leaned towards it, the faster the tapping. This time, my eyes were drawn toward the left side of his bed. I got on all fours to duck down to the lowest point of the bed, just a foot or so away from the bed frame. Was it trying to communicate with me? Head first, I slowly inched toward of the bed. The tapping got faster as I got closer; my heart was in rapid fire mode. *Tap, tap, tap,* in a fast pace, then it stopped without warning.

I cautiously, slowly lifted the sheet to see what was making the tapping sound. Every cell in my body was telling my brain to run, but I had to know. Slowly, so slowly, I quickly noticed something amiss.

'What the hell?' It looked like a white glove, like the type a golfer would use. I slowly extended my arm to reach for the glove, but before I could get it, an unseen force yanked it away from me. I jerked my hand back as fast as humanly possible. The glove landed outside my reach close to the wall. "What the fuck?" I mumbled, trying to get a better look at the glove. To my horror, at that instant, the fright I felt was like a jolt of electricity running up my back. It wasn't a glove at all, but a white bony hand attached to nothing but darkness. I broke out in goose flesh at what I just witnessed, trying to contain my scream. There was no way the hand was attached to an arm or a body. Since the bed was a twin size, there was no way a grown man could fit under the bed frame.

The fingers were skinny and almost transparent. Each finger seemed weathered, and the decay had stretched the skin to the point that bone was visible. Each digit had a long black nail, like a fang. The bleached white fingers lifted and started that frantic *tap, tap, tap,* pace on the wooden floor.

Suddenly, the hand stopped moving. In the blink of an eye, it sprang like a spider – so fast I didn't see it move – with the middle and index fingers acting like fangs, it leapt at my face. I exploded onto my backside, raising my hands to prevent that mutant from reaching my face. I landed out of its reach, but it started pulling itself toward me, grasping at the air around my leg. Then it stopped again and just like an insect, it scuttled back into the darkness under the bed. The sound of its nails clawing along the wooden floor made me shudder and doubt my sanity.

I jumped on Frank's bed like a cat. I looked down at the bottom of the bed half expecting the hand to fly up after me. Instead, I saw the back of someone's head with blue skin. Then red, blue, and purple colors... I couldn't process what I was witnessing. Out of nowhere, the head did a 360-degree turn and looked straight at me. Opaque white eyes and yellow teeth, it smiled at me as we locked eyes. I heard the word "Mine!" rasp from its mouth. Kind of like a Pez dispenser, minus the cartoon head, it contorted backwards as it slid under the bottom of his bed.

Frank was unconscious and being attacked by something, causing him to toss and thrash. I didn't want any part of that thing underneath the bed touching me. I folded my limbs so no part of me hung over the edge.

I then heard a sound coming from the wall between Frank and the bed. I peeked over between the crack when that hideous face appeared between the wall and the bed. Those white, lifeless marbles stared up at me with such venom it radiated to my bones. It slowly faded away into the darkness under the bed. Abruptly, the hand reappeared from the other side of the bed while I was facing the wall. I sensed utter malevolence as I felt it crawl up the sheets. To my shock, I was paralyzed, like an invisible force was holding me down. Distracted by the eyeball, it had had a chance to grab me when I wasn't looking.

Instantly, the hand grabbed my ankle in vice grip force. I let out a quiet scream from the pain. Then it slowly crawled up my calf, its nails digging into my skin. I tried desperately to move any part of my body, but still could not. Frank's terror continued so he couldn't help me.

That's when I saw it – a black shadow. At first, it was just a black ball. It grew into the shape of an unholy man-like thing. It had no discernable features, only darkness. The entity was pure evil and hovering above Frank. It morphed into the shape of what appeared to be a man wearing a hospital gown. As the entity floated over Frank's chest, I looked down and the hand was gone. The shadow's features became those of an emaciated old man that drifted inches away from Frank's body, now gripping his shoulders.

The entity turned to face me and pointed its bony finger at me, shouting "Mine!" It was letting me know that I had no place in this house. Frank belonged to him and there was nothing I or anyone else could do.

"Please, leave him alone," I tried to scream, but it was only a whimper.

I had learned previously that the best thing to reverse the power struggle is to curse at an entity, and much as one is able, *never* show fear. So again, I commanded, "Leave Frank alone, asshole." The more

I thought about the situation, the madder I became. I began hurling every curse word I knew. The thing smiled at me, taunting.

"I am *not* afraid of you." The angrier I got, the more control I regained of both mind and body. I stood up. As soon as I did this, the thing flew out the window like something had jerked it out using a hook.

"Get out of here!" Frank stopped flailing. "You're not welcome here," I continually repeated, as I uninvited the entity from Frank's house.

When I had full control of my body, I quickly splashed some salted water over the windowsill. I had asked Frank to make a saltwater solution before I got back from visiting Shelly. In my family, we discovered that salted water sprinkled onto windowsills and door thresholds helps prevent evil spirits from entering a dwelling. I yelled into the darkness again, "You're not welcome here." I heard a moan come from outside. It sounded like an angry man whimpering in pain.

Its angry voice cried out in my head, "It's your fault. I hate you!"

I finally knew what the entity was and how to deal with it. I had seen my Aunt Nico do a cleaning ritual at my grandmother's house and knew that was what was needed. The demon began shaking the window with a force of a small earthquake. I thought the windowpane would shatter.

Frank woke up, confused by the noise, and asked, "What's going on?"

I yelled at Frank to run and get an egg and a cup of water. Without questioning, me he sprinted into the kitchen and brought me the items I requested, including a candle with the image of a saint on the glass. It was great luck that one of the many pillars had the image of St. Michael, the Archangel. We gathered everything in the middle of the room. I lighted the candle and sat next to Frank.

"Should we hold hands?" Frank asked.

"No, just sit here and don't move." I knew it was a matter of time before the demon returned, so I had to be quick. My hands shook with anxiously and I began to sweat. I did the egg ritual, in which the egg is dropped into the water and broken. I dribbled the solution over Frank so that it covered his back, front and head; the entire intervention was done while praying.

During the ritual, we heard crying, banging, and screaming coming from the outside. I could also hear wicked laughter from a distance. A light sobbing and cursing came next. The more the ritual progressed, the less the noise. Finally, all the demonic noises stopped.

The scent of fresh flowers filled the room. The room became brighter, lighter, and warmer once the abundance of dark energy had dissipated. By this point, I was beyond tired. I was physically, mentally, and spiritually exhausted and couldn't keep my eyes open. I had never performed that ceremony before tonight. I didn't realize what a grueling a toll would be required.

I had seen my aunt Nico do this ritual on her clients many times. She was what you would call a witch, or what we call *curandera*, or healer. My aunt explained to me that it was possible to remove evil energy from a person by using an egg in a cup. Something deep inside told me I needed to do this. I knew the ritual would help my friend. I sat in the darkness listening carefully and heard nothing. It was gone.

"It's over. It worked and the demon is gone," I explained.

"It was no demon. I think maybe it was my grandfather," Frank responded.

'No way can a grandparent hate a grandchild that much,' I thought. I knew his theory was impossible because what I felt and saw was not human. He went on to explain that his grandfather had hated him since the minute he was born. "Why?" I asked. According to him, his grandfather blamed Frank's birth for Frank's *father's* downfall. Frank explained that his father married his mother without regard to what *his* father thought, so the grandfather never forgave either son or grandson. Since Frank was the oldest child, his grandfather hated him the most.

"My grandfather blames me for everything, including my father dropping out of school. He never forgave any of my family." He sighed and went over to his bed to lie down.

"Move over," I told him. There was no way I was going to sleep on the floor now. After a night of fighting with a demon, I was exhausted. 'I am never doing that shit again,' I told myself. That demon was strong enough to have either hurt me or killed me at any time. I was lucky, and I also realized that I wasn't an exorcist. I leave it to the professionals now.

In the morning, Frank was a new person. He had gone through a spiritual metamorphosis, but in the end, we both had changed. Frank had become more confident and, I shit you not, taller. He never mentioned his grandfather again. He soon became more active in school and socially, changing his life for the better.

I like to think that every child is loved by all family members, but that was not the case for my friend. I learned that hate can transcend death and the only way to correct the problem is to exorcise the evil. I also learned that the devil is not only real, but can hurt you. I never spent the night at Frank's house again, but I did visit, just to see Shelly. Frank and I sometimes ran into each other and we'd give each other a nod. I want to say this was the last time I exorcised a demon for a friend, but it wasn't.

CHAPTER 8
The Mountain of the Dead (1993)

W HEN WILL BOYS stop being boys and become men? Sometimes a traumatic experience transforms a such a boy into a man. Going to Mexico had become a burden in our social life, so my brother and I decided never to go back to Mexico for our yearly vacation. We had experienced too many bad paranormal episodes and not enough fun ones to keep us interested. Life was too short to waste on a lame vacation. Girls and having fun took priority over everything else. This was never an easy trip, but my family felt it was necessary to make the annual pilgrimage to our family's village of San Felipe. Before we could say "*Hasta la vista*, Mexico," my parents decided Juan, Jr. and I would be part of this family trip, so we hesitantly agreed.

We began our trip like we always did, waking up at 4 a.m. and climbing aboard our SUV. It was a 1983 Chevy Blazer: two doors, eight cylinders, white camper top, chrome bumpers, extra-large rims, and a jet-black paint job. I must admit, it looked badass. We somehow managed to cram my grandparents, cousins, and immediate family into one vehicle, so you can understand why we hated the traveling part our vacations – even though we had a sweet ride. To my brother and me, the thought of spending fourteen hours in a cramped, uncomfortable space, while we could have been enjoying ourselves in the comfort of our own house...well, there were better situations.

The usual drive time from Dallas to Laredo was about 7 hours until reaching the U.S.-Mexico border. Once we reached the border, I switched seats with my mother. I did this because I could not sleep while my dad was driving. I chatted to keep him company and make sure he didn't fall asleep. I enjoyed this part of the road trip because it allowed time for my father and me to bond. He liked to drive straight through the night so we could arrive in the morning. This part of the journey was also the most dangerous leg of the trip, especially driving over the mountains at night. We had to take narrow roads along mountain paths without any guardrails for protection.

We had been driving for about four hours and the radio clock read 3:10 a.m. By the way, we were traveling during the *witching* hour, a six-hour timeframe that begins at the stroke of midnight. We just arrived in the mountains around San Luis Potosi. The terrain was a mixture of desert in the valley, where we had just crossed, and forest as one ascended further up the mountains. From this point on, the roadway was extremely narrow and full of potholes that were large enough to damage our tires. My father, especially vigilant now, was driving over "*La mountaine de la muerte*," or what the locals called the mountain of death. The reason for the slang was the high volume of fatalities every year on this stretch. Besides the dangerous roads, I feared this area because of paranormal activity. Locals had told me the area was haunted by ghosts and demons; this raised my stress level even higher.

We slowly traversed the mountain, making sure we drove in the middle of the road. Illuminated along the side of the mountain, we noticed a collection of small elaborate alters that were decorated with crosses and saints.

"Someone died there," my father explained, as he pointed at one alter. "This was a whole family. They must have fallen off the mountain, poor souls." I grimaced, then looked over on my side of the road and saw the drop-off, straight down. I couldn't even see the bottom because a fog had rolled in.

"Shit Dad, should we stop and wait till this fog clears?" I asked. He looked at me like I was joking.

"You're funny," he replied. That's when we noticed headlights coming around the mountain in our direction. "I better put my high beams on so he can see us," he commented.

"I think it's a bus, Dad," I whispered. My voice cracked from the stress, but I wasn't sure what we had really seen. We saw the vehicle moving slowly into the side of the mountain and then disappear into a curve. My father drove the SUV to the right side of the road. Usually, an incoming vehicle would flash his headlights back to acknowledge they saw you, but we hadn't gotten a response back. I could see my old man was worried. He sat up straighter in his seat. He flashed the lights again, but no answer. By this time, the fog had consumed the road and the drive was treacherous.

"Dad, should we pull over and wait for the fog to pass?" I asked again. This time he didn't respond. I could tell he was nervous because his eye began twitching as the headlights came ever closer.

"There is no place to pull over," he replied, with concern in his voice. He was correct. To the right of us was a rock wall and to the left was a 100-foot drop to the valley below. The fog had thickened. I noticed what looked like shadows dancing all around the vehicle. One shadow traveled through the mist like a whale in the ocean. Maybe these things were a type of silent portent, warning us of impending doom if we continued this road. I was getting nervous, because if we pulled over, someone might run into us from behind, but if we continued, we would most definitely collide head-on with the bus.

By this time, we had lost sight of the bus. We were climbing even higher to reach the summit and visibility was sketchy, at best. My father turned up the volume on the radio. We had been listening to a local radio station playing northern style Mexican music. I had tried to switch the station since we arrived in Mexico, but my father refused. He had a tendency, when under stress, to turn up the volume. I didn't mind, now.

From a distance, we both noticed a light on the side of the road. My dad slowly rolled to a stop to see what it was. It was a man dressed in, we thought, a dated police officer's uniform, the type one would see in old nineteen twenties classic movies. I couldn't make out his face in the darkness and fog. The few details I could discern were a gray conductor style hat and matching gray jacket. The coat had a number of shiny black buttons and a white strap with red stitching that ran across his shoulders, giving an impression of an official or military capacity.

He carried an old-fashioned oil lantern, the type a train conductor would use from the 1800s. He held the lantern near his head, drawing my attention to his mustache. It was reminiscent of the type one would see on a villain in old black and white silent movies. This man looked completely out of place as he called us forward with a gesture of his arm. It seemed like the fog followed his movements, as though creating a hypnotic wave.

'What is he? Or, what could he be?' I asked myself. At the time, I didn't care. I was more worried about our head-on with the bus. He was directly in front of us now, and the lantern light radiated so brightly that neither of us could see his face.

He gestured with his lantern for us to move on the left side. At this point, we had no choice. Relief overcame my father. He had been white-knuckled steering in almost zero visibility, which ended as he followed the traffic conductor's guidance. My father, slowly, without thinking twice, moved the Blazer through the mist.

My old man yelled at the officer, "Do you mean this way, sir?" as we got closer to the unknown stranger. There was no response. My father was perturbed that he didn't get a reply. He was troubled because it might have been a trap set up by thugs to make an easy score. We were in Mexico, after all, and this situation was already dangerous.

Suddenly, we heard a loud horn and saw two headlights in front of us. The lights blinded us instantly. My father swiftly threw one arm across my chest and with his other, yanked the steering wheel in the direction of the conductor's light, pressing the gas pedal. The engine came alive as it rumbled and the tires burned rubber. The movement was so rapid we both screamed. I braced for the impact of vehicle-hitting-body and closed my eyes as we drove straight through the man. There was zero room to avoid hitting him.

Immediately before we would have felt the sickening thud, we heard a loud *zo-o-o-o-om* noise, followed by a terrible rumble that violently rocked the truck. A large, gray blur zoomed by us, inches from the Blazer. The enormous bus had come out of nowhere. My father thought the bus was going to crash into us and yelled "*Aye guey!*" in a tone I'd never heard before. For the first time, I saw real, heart-stopping fear in my father's eyes. The bus came so close we could smell the exhaust from its tailpipe. We both screamed and he lost control of the Blazer for a second, plowing down the side of the road away from the bus. There was no way the man could have possibly moved out of the way. Panicked, I imagined all kinds of crazy scenarios and one of them being, 'Will we go to jail?' As my brain reeled, Dad and I made eye contact.

Abruptly, the Blazer jarred to a stop, unsettling passengers and packed items. Everyone awoke. Everyone screamed. Then everything went quiet. The only sound breaking the silence was the Mexican music playing on the radio.

"What happened?" everyone demanded to know, in unison. My mother screamed the loudest. Her ear-splitting volume echoed in the truck as she yelled out, "What the fuck?"

My father and I, without saying a word, quickly jumped out to investigate and do a damage assessment. We knew what we saw and we knew what we had done.

"Look under the truck! Do you see him?" he desperately screamed at me. He disappeared behind the huge tire.

"Do you see anything?" I called out to him. I knew he wanted me to help him look, but I wasn't that brave. I just stood there in shock, frozen in fear, because I knew for a fact we hit the man.

The fog was remained thick, to the point I couldn't see farther than a few feet away, from any direction. It also didn't help it was still too dark to see anything. We both knew it was dangerous to be on the side of the road, especially if no one could see us. The only illumination came from our headlights and open-door lights, since there were no other vehicles and the mountain road didn't have streetlights.

The Mexican music was abruptly turned off by my grandfather

as he made his way to the front seat. As he got out of the truck, he demanded to know, "What the hell happened?" [Spanish?] My father just asked him to get back in the Blazer and that everything was alright.

"You gave your mother a fright!" [Spanish?] he screamed at my father, scolding him, like a parent to a child.

My father responded by screaming back, "DAD! Get the fuck in the car, NOW!" My grandfather, taken aback, quickly complied with his demand and got back in. His son had reached a level of agitation he had never seen before. My father was a kind, passive man, so when my grandfather heard his son shouting at him, he knew it was serious. Dad also had expectations for me now – to be a man. The reality was, I wasn't ready. I took a quick look at my family and they all nodded that I could handle this situation. I didn't want them to get out and help me look for the stranger, it was too dangerous. Besides, I had no choice.

'Is this what it takes to be considered a real man?' I wondered. I couldn't get the image of a mangled body and contorted limbs out of my head. 'No child should ever be asked to look for a dead body.'

Again, my father yelled at me, "Look under the truck." I heard him desperately search the other side of the street. "He might be alive," he yelled out. The thought of finding a severely mutilated bloody body underneath the murkiness of our truck made me want to retch. I slowly dropped to my knees to look. The smell of scorched rubber and hot brake fluid made my eyes water.

"Do you see anything?" he screamed out again.

I quickly replied, "No, I can't see past the fog." My father suggested calling out to the stranger and reaching under the truck.

"Put your hands out and feel for him," he demanded.

I wanted to say "Hell no," but if there was a chance we might be able to help him, it was worth trying. "Can you hear me? Are you alright?" I screamed out into the haze. I thought I heard a faint whimper coming from the rear of the Blazer. I was momentarily relieved. "I think I hear him," I yelled back at my dad.

"Are you serious?" he shouted back.

"Yes, please God, he might still be alive," I said. My father begged me to try again, so I closed my eyes and took a breath. I overextended my arm so much that I heard my joints crack and pop while reaching underneath the truck. My skin rubbed over the rocks and pebbles that lined the road, and the short blades of grass that had sprouted. I desperately tried to feel for anything that would indicate his presence – dead or alive.

"Are you alright? Can you hear me?" I could hear my father from the other side of the truck. I dug my toes into the road and pushed forward to stretch even farther under the SUV. Straightaway, I felt a slippery hand grab my arm, locking on like a vice grip, nails digging into my skin.

'Oh, shit!' I screamed in my head, as I was being pulled underneath the Blazer. I had lost the ability to speak. I couldn't make a sound to alert my father, much less a sentence. Hell, I was past the ability to form a coherent thought. I resisted as much as I could, but the pebbles acted like a primitive log skid – zero traction. I was going under. The thought of a bloody ghoul pulling me to its mouth, teeth snapping, salivating for a taste of my flesh, made my head want to explode. I fought back as much as I could, but it was futile. Brute force tugged at my arm and I slowly started to disappear. Instinct kicked in and I reached around to clutch anything in a desperate attempt to save myself. I tried to free my arm, but strength alone wasn't enough and my endurance had quickly faded. I was giving in to my potential demise.

The roadway became slicker the farther I got pulled underneath the vehicle. A familiar odor filled my nose when the smell of iron penetrated my nasal cavity. 'It's blood,' I thought, as I got pulled closer and closer to the undead corpse. I was covered from head to toe in thick, sticky warm ooze.

"Help, Help," I screamed for my dad, the desperate words finally formed. I kept my eyes closed. I didn't want to see what had grabbed my arm. The thick liquid now covered my face and neck. I imagined a fiendish zombie pulling me into its maw, so I closed my eyes even tighter. Any minute now, I would feel this monster tear into my flesh.

"Open your eyes, *pendejo*," that voice I heard, it was my dad. He pulled me out thinking I was the officer. He was covered in old transmission fluid from the puddle on the road. A quiet calm came over me when I realized I was going to live.

"We hit the officer head on. I am sure of it," he avowed, raising his hands in confusion. He looked at me for validation that he wasn't going mad. We thought it best not to tell the others, especially fearing ridicule from my grandfather. "Don't say anything about what happened to any of the family," he implored. It would be between us two men, and jutting his chin, sealed our agreement.

'Finally, my father considers me a man,' I thought, as I sighed and gave him a relieved smile. Nodding again, we agreed on what we witnessed and went back around the Blazer. We decided to take turns standing by the truck, hoping the injured man would find us, in case he was still alive. After my watch, I got back in the truck and drifted to sleep. The next thing I remembered was seeing daylight.

After the fog had lifted, we found ourselves parked in an ocean of makeshift altars and crosses spread out in every direction. Each altar contained a picture of a person or family. In the midst of all the memorials was a small church about the size of a chicken coop. An iron cross was perched on top of the tiny building, which had a bench in the middle fitting up to four people. The pink walls were nine feet high and enclosed with light blue iron doors. A golden statue of Jesus Christ on the cross was the centerpiece of the small building. Several paintings of the Virgin Mary and other saints adorned the other wall. The cramped church looked old but clean, its windows and floors well maintained.

'What an awkward place to put a church,' I thought. I asked my father why someone would build a church on top of a mountain by the side of a road that would barely fit two cars. He explained the church was for travelers that crossing the dangerous mountain. Some people wanted to stop and pray for safe passage before ascending to the top of the peak. Back in the old days, the road was narrower and there were no guardrails to prevent autos from tumbling over the cliffs.

"What do you think happened to that man?" I demanded to know. My father raised his hands and gave me the universal shrug for 'I don't know.' We took the time to pray at the altar and gave thanks to the man who saved our lives, then continued our journey over the mountain.

I never heard my father mention the event again except when drinking with friends. That event created a bond between my father and me that we still share to this day. I'm not sure if that experience made me a man, but I can tell you one thing, whenever I travel anywhere now, I think of the night and how a ghost saved my family.

In retrospect, I believe the ghost may have been one of the first victims when the road was but a narrow path. I have learned from the experience that not all paranormal events are the same and there is still some good, even in the afterlife.

CHAPTER 9
Army of the Dead (1993)

MEXICO IS A land of mystery and enchantment, both beautiful and ancient, with something dark in every corner. As stunning as the nation of Mexico is, the valley area is stained with Indian and Spanish blood. The town of San Felipe, our destination, still bears the scars of war on its walls and in local legends. The full name of the town is San Felipe Torres Mochas, in honor of King Phillip II of Spain, and is located northwest region of the State of Guanajuato. The township, founded in January 21, 1562 before being colonized, was part of the Aztec Empire. The valley area became a battlefield during the Chichimeca War, which lasted forty years in the late 1500s.

The Spanish had set up an army fort in San Felipe to protect their trade routes from the Chichimeca Indians. Later, San Felipe would be in the center of the Mexican War for Independence in the early 1800s. The revolutionary built tunnels underneath their homes and streets to avoid capture from the Spanish.

Still today, residents are discovering artifacts of past wars while renovating their homes. My grandfather's house was originally part of an old Spanish military fort. Our section of the building faced the main entrance into town. Rumor has it, our home was used as a courtroom, and the garden, in the middle of the house, was used for executions – well, that's what we heard.

This trip to Mexico was our last vacation as a family. As I mentioned earlier, Juan and I had decided that this would be our final crusade to San Felipe. As a child, I loved vacations there, but my priorities had changed. As a teen, I no longer wanted to visit the family home place, at least that's what I told myself, but deep in my soul, I knew I would miss the old town.

There were too many adventures to recall throughout the years. My brother and I had been habitually attacked by ghost clowns, zombie children, and other undead creatures, during past trips. Luckily, we had two sets of grandparents in San Felipe so we were able to stay at Mother's old family home place this trip. There was no way in hell I was going to remain at my grandfather's home, especially after what happened with the zombie ghost clown years back.

Juan and I were ready to get out and explore after arriving in San Felipe. The houses in the area had distinct colors: hot pinks, oceans of blues, and vibrant yellows – quite beautiful. The road in front of our maternal grandparents' house was paved with old, grey cobblestone, typical of old Spanish towns. These roads are unchanged for the past 400 years and still bear the original Spanish colonial design. My brother and I had walked those streets countless times, passing the enormous Indian statue that greeted the visitors coming into town, as we walked to *El Centro*, or downtown.

"Don't step on that," Juan laughed, as we passed horse droppings, our noses wrinkling. At the next block, the pungent air was replaced with the enticing aroma of spiced meat. The sleepy village came to life with the sounds music on every corner and car horns challenging in the background. The day was so beautiful. I wasn't sure why, but it was almost magical.

Before dark, we made sure we were home. San Felipe looked eerie as dusk approached. When it got dark, street shadows came out. Something about the way those shadows seemed to follow us… Ghost stories and urban legends filled my head, as we made our way home. After all, San Felipe was very haunted.

We had always been told that ghosts follow us home at night, so we walked faster as the night arrived. Mom's grandparents' house was directly in the middle of the neighborhood. Unlike Dad's grandparents' house, this one was smaller and had an open design. The bedrooms were on the left side of the house and the kitchen was in the back.

Next to the house was an enormous empty lot. Our next-door neighbor had claimed that it was used for public executions. Traitors and criminals had been hung from an enormous tree located in the middle of the property. We visited his house and commented on the bullet holes in one wall. He explained that back when the Spanish ruled, they used this wall for the firing squad.

'No way,' we thought. It turned out to be true.

What had always scared us was the old tree. It was colossal, like a pyramid, and wide enough to easily climb. The limbs stretched out over our house and wall, with foot-long green leaves hanging from each branch. A lesion near the base looked like an open mouth, ready to accept alms or sacrifices. At night, I would run past the long pointed leaves that looked more like fingers, reaching for me.

The townspeople claimed the *lechusa* would sit on top of the branches and snatch kids as they passed under it. *Lechusa* is a witch with a woman's head and a body of an owl. She was blamed for children disappearing while they slept. It didn't help at night that the branches would scratch the top of the house, like a cat clawing at the door.

On this particular night, there was a wicked wind blowing down from the mountain. We heard a low-pitched moan that came from the direction of the ancient tree.

"Here comes the dead," one kid muttered, as he jokingly pointed at the vacant lot. Most teens in the area took the paranormal seriously, especially *that* tree. Juan and I finished playing soccer on the street with some locals when we got back from the village. When they realized we lived next to the vacant lot, they casually asked us if we had ever have seen a ghost in our grandparent's house. I responded with a confident "No," as we walked into our house.

Our room was adjacent to the front door, and like most Mexican households, all the doors were made of metal. One thing we hated about our room was how easily sound traveled from passing cars and talking people from the street. I'm not sure if the door helped amplify the sound because of the metal or our teenage nerves, but the sounds kept us up all night. My brother and I slept on a queen sized bed on the far right side of the small room.

"Let's go to bed," my brother called to me. We already had dinner at a taco stand that was near the Indian statue. It had been a busy day, and we were tired from exploring and playing. My parents weren't staying at this house. We had split up and they stayed at my paternal grandfather's house, which was more spacious than where we staying.

My grandparents' bedroom was located next to the kitchen at the far end of the house. I never liked the fact that it was so far from us. Our room was creepy. It reminded me of a crypt because of the cement walls. I am a light sleeper so any noise would wake me. I claimed the left side of the bed next to the wall; Juan liked staying closer to the door. We both quickly fell asleep as the wind blew through the halls of the residence. Oddly, the constant scratching from the tree didn't bother us that night.

I woke up around four in the morning hearing a drumline, *Brrum! Brrum, brrrumble, ba-dOnk-a-dOnk*. 'What in the heck is that noise?' I wondered. It sounded like the staccato pattern that an army drumline would play. I woke up my brother.

"Do you hear that?" he put his ear up in the air. Instantly, we heard what sounded like a high school band horn. "Is there a band marching outside coming this way?" He asked me like I knew the answer. "No, that's crazy," I answered. We stayed quiet to figure out what was going on. We could hear people from the street speaking classic Castilian Spanish, not the type you hear in current Mexico vernacular.

We both got up and made our way to the door. *Brrum! Brrum, brrrumble, ba-dOnk-a-dOnk*. The drumming sounded closer and louder. The room began to quake from the vibrations, like sounds from hundreds of footsteps marching in unison.

"They must be marching into San Felipe from the mountain," we both whispered, agreeing. Immediately, we heard voices next to our residence.

"*Buscalos, estan aqui,*" "Look for them, they're here somewhere," someone shouted. The sound of doors being broken down and people screaming filled our ears. We started to panic as we realized they were searching for someone.

"What's going on?" we whispered in disbelief, retreating to corner of our bed. Not saying anything, we sat in the darkness listening to the army outside, hoping they would go away.

"*Abran la puerta.*" "Open the door," the voices of angry men echo in the night. *Brrum! Brrum, brrrumble, ba-dOnk-a-dOnk.* The drumline echoed outside our room.

"*Aqui, aqui,*" Here, here," a man screamed from the other side of the door.

"Shit, help me," my brother pleaded. We leapt from the bed to barricade our bedroom door.

Bang, bang, pop, pop, hearing the savage shooting that demanded entry into the house. The courtyard door just opened without anyone opening it. We heard several men walk into the courtyard.

"They're inside our house now. How was it possible?" we asked ourselves. Our bedroom door was locked and barricaded, so there was no way they could get inside. My brother and I hid behind the bed. We could hear the soldiers walking towards our room. The light from their lantern shone at the bottom of the door. The drums began to move down the street again as we heard the voices of men from a distance.

"Open the door," someone shouted aggressively from the other side of the door.

I told my brother, "Hurry up, open the door before they knock it down,"

Juan said "No! Are you stupid? Let them try to knock down a metal door. They'll break their legs before they manage to open our bedroom door." So we waited in the darkness and hid behind the bed. *Bang! Bang! Bang! Pop!*

"*Aberie la puerta*," "Open the door," someone commanded from the other side of the door, demanding we obey. We were frozen, fearing whatever was outside.

"Stay quiet," Juan whispered. The door rattled and clanged like a bell with every blow. *Bang, bang.* Then we heard a rooster crowing as sunlight beamed under the door. Our room suddenly became normal again; all we could hear was the calm silence of the morning. We looked at each other confused.

"Did we dream everything?" we asked each other. We slowly opened the door and saw nothing but the old tree and long branches looming over the side of the wall.

"Let's go!" my brother shouted, as he ran to my grand parents' room. I quickly followed, only to discover they were gone. Both my grandparents were already up and drinking coffee in the kitchen. Quickly, we explained what we experienced during night.

"We heard an army marching through the streets last night, Grandmother. Then they knocked on our door." My grandmother, without saying a word, looked at my grandfather.

"*Son los muertos del arbol*," "They are the dead from the tree," he said, pointing to the tree over his wall. "They hung many people from that particular branch, both rebels and civilians, alike. The Spanish army would come at night and drag the townspeople out of their homes and hang them if they were thought to be traitors." He explained how many of the rebels would build secret underground rooms to hide from the armies. Many times, innocent people suffered from senseless searches and hung for being related to the accused traitor. My grandfather explained, "It was the army of the dead and they always come at night. If you don't open the door, you will be okay," he explained.

We asked, "Does this happen all the time?"

He replied, "Not all the time, only to certain people. You can sleep with us tonight." As they made us breakfast he said, "Don't worry, the dead never bother us." Juan and I blinked.

We ended up spending the remainder of our summer sleeping in our grand parents' room. If you ever visit San Felipe, never open the door when someone is knocking at night. It might be the army of the dead coming to hang you from the old tree. To this day, the old tree is a gruesome reminder of San Felipe's tragic and murderous past. Don't get me wrong, Mexico is a beautiful land. It's worth a visit.

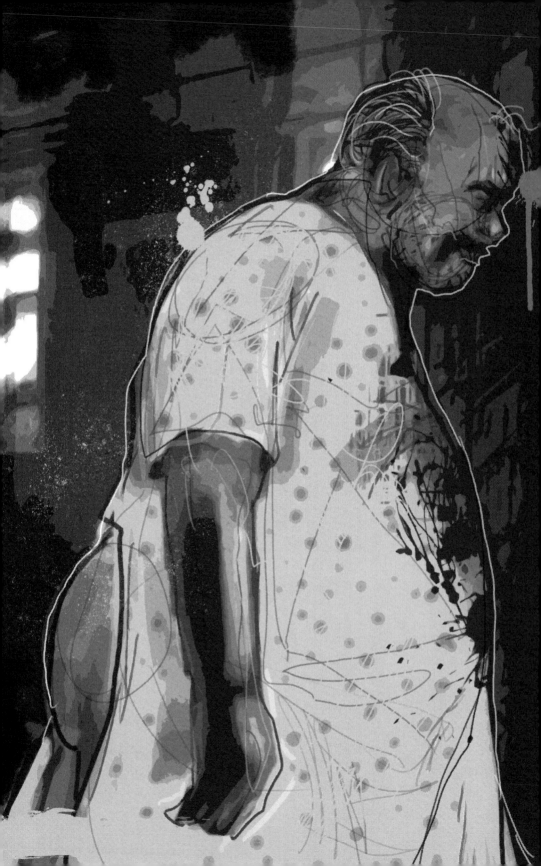

CHAPTER 10
It Lurks in the Basement (1996)

WHAT CAUSES A place to be haunted? First of all, it needs to have a history of tragedy and death. Second, the location must be historic. Third, the structure must be emotionally draining due to those tragedies and deaths. The only places that consistently match all three criteria are hospitals. I know beyond doubt that every hospital I have ever visited has been haunted. But only one hospital stands out, so far, as having the most paranormal activity.

Being a psychic medium and working around death wasn't a career option, but my dream was to become a doctor and I wasn't going to let anything stand in my way, not even the dead. After high school, I got a job as a technician in an Emergency Pharmacy Department. We supplied medications to all the higher acuity areas of the hospital, like the Emergency Department (ED), Intensive Care Units (ICU), etc. Because the pharmacy operated 24/7, it had to be staffed 24 hours round the clock. So, I was hired to work the night shift – not great, but I thought this would be a good job to cut my teeth on before going to college, and eventually medical school.

This wasn't your typical pharmacy. As the department title implied, we provided adjunct care for emergency situations. When a medication order came in, our team prepared the drugs and returned them via a pneumatic tube system from the basement. Only for certain emergencies did we techs personally hand-deliver the narcotics or specialty meds to the ED. When I got such a notification, my job was to push a locked medication cart as fast as I could to the requesting trauma room. If I didn't move quickly enough, a patient might die, so being late was not an option.

By law, I could only release narcotics after obtaining a doctor's signature; then release them to the head trauma nurse. It was common to walk into the middle of an emergency surgery, as I discovered during day shift orientation. These procedures were done mostly for bullet wounds or something else equally intense. Only a few times did I arrive too late… the patient had already passed away.

This was one of many reasons why my job was so stressful. Not only did we have to be fast, but sometimes I was asked to act as a translator because most hospitals ran a skeleton crew at night. This hospital was in a lousy neighborhood in south Dallas, so most of our patients were poor Latinos or another minority. Since I'm fluent speaking Spanish, I was regularly asked to translate messages from the doctors to patients, and sometimes the family, and many times it was not good news.

After I began orientation to night shift, I was told to avoid and report, in case a suspicious person was spotted. One of the hazards of our department, when hand-delivering medications, was drug addicts roaming the dark hallways. The reality of the situation was that our night security team consisted of old, retired police officers who had a habit of sleeping in their office. This meant we were pretty much on our own at night. What made it worse? Our power-saving program designed to save money. The hospital used a motion sensor system to conserve energy at night. This meant the hallways stayed dark most of the night, making our jobs hazardous, as well as dangerous.

Our only lighting at night was cast from an exit sign in the middle of the hallway. We had to move vigorously to activate the sensors. Most of the time, even leap-frogging wouldn't turn them on. Maybe it was because we were in the basement in the old part of the hospital. Regardless, the perpetual darkness that consumed the hallways was creepy. Just imagine pushing a cart through a pitch-black corridor, and the only thing guiding you is a buzzing, red exit sign.

The creep factor increased because the morgue was located next to our pharmacy. Any expired patients, brought over by hospital staff, were stored overnight until the mortuary or the Medical Examiner picked them up the next morning. This meant that we were mostly alone in the basement – all night. No big deal, right? No… not exactly. It was apparently common knowledge that ghosts haunted the basement. Not one particular ghost, but I was told there were several reported throughout the years.

After several days of orientation, tonight was my first night to work an abbreviated graveyard shift. The night started out slow and I had just completed all my tasks. We would routinely start each shift by preparing the neonatal feeding bottles and work on some chemo bags for the ICU's. My anxiety over being alone had just subsided and I wanted to relax for the rest of the night. My feet hurt, so I sat down to rest and wait for *stat* and special orders from the ED. It was 2:03 in the morning and just two more hours before I could go home.

Out of the blue, the phone rang and a special order arrived in the queue. The pharmacist on duty with me was a cute, petite red head from Louisiana. She was fresh out of pharmacy school and new to the hospital and midnight shift. Naturally, since had I prayed for a slow night, an order dropped into the pneumatic tube station.

"We have a trauma order," she shouted. I gathered the orders and drugs and waited for her to double check and verify the medications, then loaded the med cart. Before rushing outside, I reviewed the checklist and location of the patient's room.

"Go, go!" she shouted. Without thinking, I started to run down the halls. Shit, I forgotten my badge. I needed my badge to access certain doors because our pharmacy was in a secured area.

As I walked swiftly back past the first hallway, that's when I noticed a patient, or at least what I thought was a patient. He was wearing a typical hospital gown, so he was almost naked. The back of the gown was open, exposing his hairy backside. I looked up, trying not to notice his hairy ass, as I walked past him. He was an obese man of Mexican descent who was standing near the wall.

The air felt colder and I sensed a dark energy follow me. I can't explain it exactly, but I got the impression of loneliness. As I walked on, I detected the smell of burned electrical wire and meat. 'What is that strange smell?' I thought. It was common to smell weird odors down here, so I didn't make a big deal of such an odor emanating from the patient.

This man faced the wall, like a child in timeout. I thought again, another oddity. It wouldn't be the first time a patient, somehow, found their way to the basement. Keeping my eyes on the stranger, I passed by him slowly, making sure to memorize his face, just in case I had to call Security. The stranger turned his head slowly towards me. We made eye contact. I noticed his blood-shot red eyes, like he'd been crying all night, sunken in a leathery weathered face that prominently featured a thick, black mustache. I nodded my head and said "*Hola*." He responded back with a slow painful nod as we locked eyes. There was no way I was going to get robbed by this dope fiend – not tonight.

'This guy is on something,' I thought to myself. Protocol dictated that I should alert my pharmacist as fast as I could, so I ran back to the pharmacy. "There's a strange man crying outside. What should we do?"

She responded with "What man?" Our office had a window for walk-up orders that faced the dark hallway.

"That person," I said, pointing my finger in the direction of the patient. "What do we do? I thought this area was secured."

"Call Security," she replied.

"No time, I've got to go," as I grabbed my ID badge and headed toward the hallway door.

"Don't leave me alone," she implored. I knew she was afraid because she would be the only person left in the pharmacy.

"I'm coming back with Security, so wait for us." She sharply nodded. I tried to make sense of how a person could make their way down to the basement without a security card. Access to the basement was almost impossible because of the multiple security doors. That meant he followed someone down here or came from the morgue.

We watched the naked man slowly limp towards the pharmacy

window. As he turned to look in our direction, his drooling mouth was opened, like he wanted to say something, but couldn't find the words. Instead, he tapped on the glass with his forehead, leaving a sweat stain. We both stepped back in fright. The stranger mouthed unintelligible grunting sounds. He slowly turned and walked deeper into the darkness.

"Call Security," she whispered, in a frightened tone.

I quickly replied, "You call them, I still need to go." I was overdue to deliver the meds. "Hide in your office and I'll be back as soon as possible," I said, ensuring I had my badge as I ran out the door. A cold blast of air hit my face when I opened the hallway door and stepped into the darkness towards the elevator. It was too dark to see down the hall where the man walked, but I had a clear path to the elevator. 'Fuck it,' I thought, making up my mind. I took off.

I was expecting to be grabbed and murdered, but nothing happened. I pushed the heavy cart across the hallway. After pressing the elevator button, I turned to look down the hall. The sound of something coming towards me got my attention. The same grunting sound came from the dark hallway. The car still hadn't arrived. I pressed the button again, willing the elevator doors open. I could hear someone slowly trudging my way.

There was nothing between me and the stranger except my med cart. I positioned the cart in front of me, in case I needed to defend myself. The motion sensors still hadn't activated the overhead lights – it was light-sucking black – so I jumped up and down to try to turn them on, but nothing happened. The grunting sounds sounded closer and louder.

The lights finally blinked on. The man continued to limp towards me, his arms extended in my direction, like an old mummy movie. He shuffled two more steps and the lights behind him went dark. He was almost at the elevator. Urgently pressing the button again and again, I finally heard the familiar ding of the door opening. My heart was pounding like a drum by this point. The door slowly opened as light from the elevator spilled across the hallway; I rushed in. The stranger was just outside the perimeter of the light, but I knew he was even closer. His silhouette appeared in the shadows as the doors slowly closed. He could have easily opened the door, but he did not.

The doors closed and car ascended to the first floor. 'Oh, my gosh, please hurry!' I thought. Still frightened, I raced out of the elevator past the newest wing of the hospital to access the Emergency Department, continued past the waiting room and into the operating room.

"Over here," a nursed called me. "I don't think we are going to need it after all," she explained, "but the doctor wants to ask you for a favor." The young doctor passed me a handwritten note and asked if I would translate his message to the family about the status of their loved ones. My first instinct was to decline because I needed to find the security officer, but I knew my pharmacist was safe in her office.

I hesitantly agreed, thinking, 'I'll make this quick. After all, I've done this before – no big deal.' So I walked into the waiting room and that's when my heart almost stopped. There were at least thirty people crammed into the small space. Everyone stopped talking and turned to listen to what I had to say. The blood rushed to my head and my vision became blurry. I struggled to speak as my nerves got the best of me. The family had a picture of a couple – someone's father and mother. The doctor's note read: "My condolences to your family. Mr. Garcia did not survive the trip to the hospital and passed away upon arrival. I am very sorry. Mrs. Garcia is still in surgery and has a chance to survive. Please pray she will make it through the night. Once we stabilize her, you may see her."

As I finished the note, the room erupted in heartbreaking crying and moaning. "Doctor, Doctor!" as they implored, wanting additional information from me. As the mob rushed toward me for answers, I slowly backed out into the hall, becoming once again, a regular pharmacy tech. I asked the young doctor who handed me the note if the woman was going to make it, and he responded "No, but you always want to give the family hope," as he walked back into the surgery room. I found out the couple had been in a horrible accident. They were driving home after visiting their grandkids in north Dallas when a drunk driver hit them head-on.

A young woman, maybe their daughter, walked out of the waiting room holding a small family picture. The photograph showed a woman in her thirties sitting next to a man, about the same age, surrounded by three kids. There were two boys and one girl; I assumed she was the little girl.

"This is the only picture I have of them," the woman sobbed, handing me the framed photograph.

I explained, "I am not a doctor. I was asked to translate his message." Once she realized I had no authority to help her, she pulled me forcefully with one arm back to the surgery room looking for the resident on duty.

"Why do you wear a white coat like a doctor?" she asked.

"I work in the pharmacy," I responded. I stood in the doorway, pleading with her, "Look, they're trying everything they can to save her, so please go back into the waiting room."

Sometimes a minority patient's family has the notion that their lives aren't worth saving, or maybe the medical staff doesn't care, but that was wrong. Truth be told, there was many a night – especially with new residents – staff are found sobbing, usually hiding in the basement where they can isolate themselves and release their own grief.

I explained, "This is a difficult profession and we're just human."

She nodded and agreed, "Tell them he was a good man." Then she thanked me for trying to help. Something about the man's face in the picture was familiar.

"Can I see the picture again?" I asked. As she handed me the old picture frame she turned around, her hand shaking.

"This was when we had just arrived here from Mexico." I felt a shiver as I recognized her father's face. "It couldn't be," as I realized the man in the picture was the same man in the dark hallway. "Holy crap – it *is* him," I thought, trying to maintain my composure.

Now I realized his grunting was more like a cry for help and that's why he followed me to the elevator. The dead man wanted me to deliver a message to them; it made sense now. "I am so sorry for your loss. Your father is in a better place," giving my condolences. She nodded peacefully, her face lighting up with a smile as she went back into the waiting room. Based on her expression, I felt like, deep inside, I had delivered his message.

I needed to get back to my pharmacist, while still following protocols for alerting Security about intruders, even though I knew it was the recently deceased soul. I made it to the Security Office, a short distance from the ED. Both security guards were asleep, as usual, with their legs propped on top of their desks. The office had a disgusting, stale odor of old gym socks and Doritos; I tried not to breathe. When I spoke, out squeaked something that sounded close to a screamed whisper, "We need your help. We have an intruder in the basement!"

The old guard slowly got up and nagged his partner up. They both started to laugh.

"You must be new to the night shift, huh?" as they cackled, laughing at me.

Embarrassed to respond, I answered, "Yes, it's my first night, why?"

"Let me guess. You saw someone in the basement, right?"

"Ummm, yes," I responded, not getting the implication.

"This isn't the first time we've been called down to the basement. We never find anything because it's a ghost," said the elderly black security guard, as he made the sign of the cross. "It happens now and then, especially with the new night shift employees." He got up and put his gun in his belt and made his way to the elevator. "I'll be back, Jones," he promised, as though making some sort of bet.

"You better pay up, brother," his partner said, laughingly.

The guard and I both ran back to the pharmacy elevator. He checked all the hallways and closets and found them empty. "I told you pharmacy people before, there's nothing down here," as he giggled and pulled a piece of gum out of his pocket. "You get used to seeing them, especially around this hour. But don't worry, they haven't hurt anyone… yet." Confused, I gave him an 'Are you shitting me?' smile.

Refusing to accept his suggestion, I countered, "Look, I know what I saw, and it was no ghost!" After we had both looked again, I apologized to the guard about the false alarm. We walked into the pharmacy and the young pharmacist almost gave him a hug.

"Did you get him?" she asked, wanting an affirmative answer.

"I am sorry Miss, he's long gone," the security guard replied. I explained that it was a false alarm, in spite of what we both knew we had seen.

Looking confused and in denial, she angrily stated, "Oscar and I *both* saw a naked man."

He replied with a smirk on his face, "I am sure you did sweetie, but there's no way we can arrest a ghost." As he walked past me, we heard him muttering to himself, "Guess I lost this bet."

"Ghost?" as the pharmacist turned to me for answers.

"Yep, it was a ghost," I explained, as she made me lock the doors and walk her to her room while she held onto my shoulders.

Confused and scared, she asked me again, "But we both saw him in the flesh, right?" as she kept repeating this to me.

All I could do was just nod in agreement. I knew who the naked man was and why he was sobbing. You see, his wife died later that night and I believe he was just waiting for her to join him in death. He wasn't the only spirit I encountered in this hospital. This confirmed to me that love *does* survive beyond death, and there is such a thing as everlasting love.

CHAPTER 11
Daemonium (1996)

B EING ABLE TO see the dead and working night shift at the community hospital wasn't the best idea. In reality, I should have known better, but as I mentioned earlier, I wanted to be a doctor and felt that working in a pharmacy benefited my goal. I continued working as a pharmacy technician for about a year after high school.

The average person would have been scared out of their mind working next to a morgue, and especially at night. I had already experienced so many insane things that I had become numb to the paranormal activity. Death was part of the job and I felt its presence around me, especially in darkened hallways in the oldest part of the hospital.

The original structure had not changed since the early nineteen hundred's, and some halls had not seen the light of day in years. The oldest section had hidden passages that only a few people knew about – security guards and the medication runners, like me. According to historical records, the older sections, built in the late 1920s, were used to house the mentally ill from the 50s through the 80s. To this day, stories are recalled that some of the patients would escape and torment the local elementary school down the street. I know this to be true.

Daemonium (1983)
Part 1: Lunatic

I ATTENDED THE old James Hogg Elementary School when I was in second grade. It was a small, low-income school attended by Mexican and black students. The distance between the school and this same hospital is about two blocks. My family lived across the street from the school, so my memory of this event haunts me and my family to this day, even now when I hear about school shootings.

I remember hearing the intercom interrupt the middle of our naptime. A smooth, deep male voice calmly told the teachers to lock the doors and turn off the lights – no explanation. I am sure the teachers were trained for emergencies, after all, we were on a bad side of town.

At the time, we had an open school, which meant all the doors remained unlocked during the day. The school administration consisted of the secretary, a nurse, a counselor, cafeteria staff, janitors, a vice principal, and the principal. The only real security was our janitor, who, on some occasions, would chase away local drug addicts that wandered into our school. This was different.

Our teacher tried to stay tranquil, not to unnerve her students, but we could see it on her face. Fear, and not just any fear, but the type that changes a person's physical and mental demeanor. The school had just posted an intruder alert, sending the school into lockdown. The secretary came to the door to speak to our teacher as soon as the message was over. She whispered to her, "Ms. Porknoid, man with a knife has been seen on the playground. Lock your door until further notice."

Our teacher closed the door and asked all us to assume the tornado drill position. Most of us kids were not aware of the situation. As she turned off the lights, begging us to be quiet, we hid under our desks. Confused by her actions, I started to get scared. Being seven years old, I didn't understand the severity of the situation.

"For the love of God, children, be silent," she whispered into the group of frightened children. We all stayed as quiet as any child could, under the circumstances, save whimpers and sniffling.

Like something out of our worst nightmare, we heard a light scraping sound coming from the other side of the wall next to the cafeteria. It was as if someone had taken a sharp stick and slowly dragged it across the wall. We followed the sound of the scraping noise as it got closer to our room.

Our classroom was the first room we entered from outdoors next to the cafeteria. The homeroom door had a frosted glass window, which was translucent enough to see people walking in the hallway. The door had our teacher's name and grade level posted one the wood. The door wasn't very thick, and the glass had broken before, so it seemed a matter of time before that happened again.

Ms. Porknoid wore sizable, thick red glasses, which were too big for her small head. We always thought her glasses matched her reddish hair. Being a heavy-set young woman, or what we called a "big-boned" southern woman, she sometimes had trouble getting around our small room. In those days, it was common to have overcrowded classes of thirty or more children in a room designed for fifteen students. The number of children made the room impossible to move around, especially for her, but not this time.

In her panic, that she had forgotten to lock the door after speaking to the secretary. Reality setting in, all the children began screaming. She jumped up and raced to the door in break-neck speed. She flew by our desk and even managed to jump over some kids to the door. The intruder, almost as if sensing her frantic intensions, also raced toward our door. Our teacher and the crazed person managed to get to the door at the same time. Luckily, Ms. Porknoid was swift enough to slide the deadbolt; we all heard the satisfying *click*. The stranger jiggled the doorknob while Ms. Porknoid held on tightly, double-checking the lock.

"Oh my gosh, please leave!" she screamed in her polite southern tone. The stranger, not responding to her request, just stood there looking toward her direction. Ms. Porknoid again demanded, this time in her most authoritative voice, the intruder to leave, "Leave! The police are coming. You're trespassing." Although the room was darkened, the hallway light shone enough that we saw her sweat uncontrollably.

Panic erupted amongst the kids as they cried and called out for their mothers. We could see a sense of dread come over our teacher's face. She took a breath and calmly fixed her glasses. She recognized the panic and implored her students to stay quiet, putting her finger over her mouth.

The man mostly stood outside the door, motionless. Intermittently, he threw himself against the door with such violence that we could hear the glass snick from stress. 'It's going to break,' my young mind thought. I instinctively looked for an escape route out of the room, but we were trapped. The classroom had no windows, so hiding was the only option. He jiggled the doorknob again and we all screamed.

We could see the shadowy outline of his body. We screamed again, when he pressed his face against the frosted glass; a lone eyeball was seen looking into the room. Ms. Porknoid stepped back in fear. He was wearing a gown – the type a patient would wear in a hospital. We couldn't distinguish his facial details clearly, but perceived he was a black male, fifty or so, with a broad frame. His hair looked wild and kinky, and it moved when he moved. We noticed he had an object in one hand like the shape of a large butcher knife. He had positioned the knife behind his back, making it visible when his body struck the door.

The doorknob jiggled wildly as the man tried to open our door again. I'm sure Ms. Porknoid realized this demented man had evil intentions. She used her body to wedge herself against the door, acting as a barrier between the mad man and her children. We could see sweat beaded over her forehead as the man repeatedly rammed the door. By some miracle, the glass did not shatter. The door remained closed.

He suddenly stopped and walked toward the next room. I could feel my heart beat out my chest as I looked around at the disarray. Ms. Porknoid slowly stepped away from the door after he left. Then we heard the next second grade class screeching, as the lunatic tried to open their door, too. The cries from next door frightened us even more than the stranger.

"Be quiet, class," commanded Ms. Porknoid, who was now physically exhausted and crying uncontrollably. The wailing exploded inside our classroom again when we saw two large shadows sprint toward the stranger.

"Get on the ground!" The sound of police sirens capped off our fright.

Ms. Porknoid had slumped against the door wearing the blank expression of someone who had seen their life flash before their eyes. I, too, had my short life flash before me, and this memory still burns my mind.

Every time I walked through the old mental ward, I wondered if this was the same demented man who had escaped this very floor, many years ago.

Daemonium (1996)
Part 2: The Beast

I HAD BECOME accustomed to the smell of death and sickness in the hospital. As an empath, I can feel a patient's pain. This always makes me sick and gives me a headache.

Back then, there were days when I could feel death hovering around the terminally ill. Whenever I walked by those patients, I could sense dark energy hiding, restlessly lurking in the shadows while it waited for a patient to die. I know this sounds morbid, but true. It felt like a predator, and this predator was aware of me.

I'd never felt anything like it before; it scared me to the core. So much so, that I feared it might follow me home. Just in case that happened, I performed my cleansing ritual before going home. This consisted of a ritual of mixing one egg into a full cup of water. I believe the dead exist in total darkness in another dimension, close to our own, and occasionally crossover to feed on people with particular energy they're attracted too. Like a beacon of light in a dark void, like moth to a flame, they follow me.

The first time I saw the creature I called "death," was when I was driving home after my shift ended –around five in the morning. I was turning right to take the main artery to the street to my house. Without warning, a bizarre pitch-black creature galloped across the street from the shopping center into the hospital garage. I rubbed my eyes just to make sure what I just witnessed. The hair on my neck stood up as I shivered. This was nightmare shit.

It appeared as a half-dog/half-cat creature with human-like features. Not a person, not an animal, or at least not anything from this world. When it ran, it traveled on all fours, like a big cat, but when it stopped or walked, it rose up on two legs. This beast wasn't huge, but more like the size of a regular person. The odd thing was that its round head had no facial features. The creature's skin had a slick, oily looking quality and was completely black. Oh, not your typical shade of black, but one that consumed all light, creating a black hole of evil.

I knew this thing had never been human. It was an ancient demonic creature that had never existed in this world. The feeling I got from it was hatred so profound that it made my skin crawl; I couldn't drive away fast enough. I remember when growing up, my father always told me not to fear the dead, because they can't hurt you. Well, I'm not sure the rules applied to whatever this entity was and I don't think it was ever alive.

This was the parasite that waited for the sick and dying, feeding on them while they slept, the same evil that sometimes passed me in the Emergency Department on my med runs. *This* was thing that I had sensed in the shadows. It noticed me – but, this thing also feared me.

I love kids, but I have a special affinity for babies. I often volunteered in the nursery to feed the newborns in the neonatal ICU before my shift and on breaks. I had a calming effect on them. Occasionally and inexplicably at night, the room would go dark. If an infant whimpered, I sensed the entity was close, so I prayed to God to keep the baby safe.

I finally understood why prayer was the key. The thing wouldn't come near people who gathered to pray. So, I began praying on my own, hoping to drive the creature away from the newborn ward. I had to do something because I felt like the innocent depended on me.

'Death is natural,' I used to tell myself. There was nothing natural about this monster. It hid from me in the shadows of the empty rooms, at least that's what I'd like to think. In reality, I had no clue if it disappeared because me, out of fear, or was waiting for a future moment to attack me. Either way, I could never show fear.

Nowadays, I always get asked why I didn't say something. How could I warn someone about this experience without sounding crazy? I couldn't, so I chose to ignore it and hope it didn't decide to follow me home.

Daemonium (1996)
Part 3: It Feeds

On this day, the hospital was quieter than usual and very empty. I was about to end my shift but still needed to work a couple of more hours before I could leave. My pharmacist tonight was another new grad from Louisiana. He was overweight with premature balding, which made him look older than he was, but nevertheless, very polite and friendly.

"We are a team. You pull the medications and I'll approve them," he explained in his southern accent. Most times, I just filled the urgent orders and placed them into a pneumatic tube for delivery to various departments in the main hospital. When narcotics were ordered, a rapid critical hand-to-hand delivery was required. After all, the situation hinged between life and death – a no-brainer – I had to run.

I liked to explore the halls on the second floor between the Emergency and Pharmacy Departments. Studying the layouts and corridors helped me find the best shortcuts through the old wards and original ED to the newer sections of the hospital. My medication runner goal: find the fastest route to any destination.

During orientation on day shift, I had discovered a shortcut through a wing that had been added on during the 1940s. Even though slated for renovation, the hallway through this old mental ward knocked about five minutes off my usual route. This section hadn't been used for patient care for many years, so it became a repository for medical equipment. Most of the empty patient rooms contained extra beds, cabinets, and over-bed tables. Overflow medical supplies were stacked in hallways and dusty waiting areas. This unit, too, had motion sensor lights.

All I needed to do was to take the service elevators to the second floor, pass through the old Emergency Room area, and down the hall through the old mental ward. I'd explored this path thoroughly, so

I was very familiar with every door and sign in the old mental ward and ER, as it was called back in the day. My previous path had been a circuitous route before reaching the new hospital ED. I wouldn't think twice about using my new shortcut during the night shift.

Ring, ring. My heart nearly beat out of my chest. 'Time to test my new route to the ED,' I thought. After the orders were double-checked, the cart was made ready and locked. I hoofed it through the dark basement into the freight elevator and punched the button to the second floor. As the second floor doors opened, I found myself enclosed in a wall of darkness that engulfed the elevator. This was a total absence of light; what I call absolute darkness. I was terrified. This was akin to diving into a lake at night with no moonlight. I started to have second thoughts about continuing this path.

I knew this old part of the hospital was very haunted, hell, everyone knew this. Walking into total darkness was worse than foolish, especially for me. Every bone in my body told me not to go into the darkness. 'Man up,' I goaded myself. 'It's too late to turn back now,' I thought. I had already wasted too much time. Thinking outside the box, I grabbed my pager and tried to use it as a small flashlight, but it didn't help.

"Fuck it," I muttered. As I dove into the darkness with the scant light from the elevator buttons, I could hear this gliding ping behind me. The elevator door was slowly closing. I could feel my heart pounding. Fired-up nerves sent tingles into my hands. Anxiously, I found myself in total blackness, coldness. I couldn't even see my hands, except for my fingers that were pinning the pager to the cart.

'Walk. You remember every sign and door in this part of the mental ward,' was the pep talk in my head. I slowly pushed my way through the darkness, knowing I had memorized the path to the other side of the old, empty emergency room. "It's not far," I said aloud, to calmly remind myself. I resumed walking through the hallway.

I instantly felt someone standing next to me. My skin burned and tingled as I turned my head to ignore the presence near me. As I walked, I felt a wall of cold air enveloping one spot of the hallway. 'Maybe it's a vent,' I rationalized, but I knew better. My skin became cold and goose-pimples burst over on my neck and arms. "Keep walking," I commanded my body.

Bam. Immediately my cart hit something in the hallway. I steered the cart out of whatever was obstructing my path. My Scooby sense kicked in, and now I knew for a fact I wasn't alone. I had felt this evil presence before in the ICU. Blood rushed to my face as I recognized its oppressing energy. I was in trouble and I knew I had no escape. The death creature had returned – for me. Of this, I was certain. Why me? Of that, I was unsure.

Like a predator, its tapping steps circled me. I felt like I was being hunted by an unnatural presence. Its low moaning and heavy, raspy breathing, and rotten, sulfurous, decaying exhalation made me gag. Its teeth were inches from my neck. It wanted to hurt me, but couldn't… it just mocked me. There was no escape now.

I turned the corner out of the old emergency room as my eyes adjusted to the darkness. I was overcome with relief after spotted the glowing red exit sign in the mental ward, my only source of visible light. Even though my eyes had adapted to the darkness, I stumbled through the hallway and noticed some of the old mental patient rooms were open. It wasn't strange to have doors ajar because they were used to store extra medical equipment and furniture. However, I didn't remember seeing these particular doors open the last time I walked through.

My stomach churned when I felt more than one entity. I turned to look toward a room located in the middle of the hallway. Without warning, I started hearing whispers and giggles all around me. I tried to ignore the voices.

"Hey, can you help me?" an older man's voice whispered across the hallway into my ears. His voice came through my ear like a vibrating radio signal. "Can you hear me?" he asked me again. My skin crawled. I knew no one was in there. "Come here," the voice demanded with a calm tone. I knew better than to invite a spirit to talk to me. I'm not stupid, so I ignored the voice and walked even faster. "COME HERE! JOIN ME!" it raged. My soul trembled while I stopped and tried to compose myself.

At this point, I started running. Speeding past another open door, I abruptly stopped when I noticed someone or something that had been lying on bed stand up. I only saw him/it for an instant, and from what I could make out, he was wearing a white or light blue patient gown. It was too dark to see his face, but his pale head seemed to radiate like the moon. I had seen this thing before but couldn't place the occasion.

There was luminescent, red-tinted slime on the face. It opened its mouth and slime spilled out, then lunged over as though in pain. The ghoul's long hair was wild, matted, and stuck out at odd angles. In the ghetto, we would call it nappy, but that's the only way I could describe its hair. Its arms were holding on to the side of the bed as it lifted itself and pointed one arm in my direction. He was holding something in his hand – a cooking knife. The entity seemed to gleam; not a bright glow, but more like a fog in the darkness. It started to stumble toward me, lost its footing, and landed behind on a chair. Then it opened its mouth one more time as it looked directly at me.

"HELP ME," it malevolently shouted. The sound of licking lips filled the darkness. A choking sound was followed by the noise of the chair being hurled violently against a wall. It was completely motionless... then catapulted towards me, leaving a trail of vomit on the floor. It was still pitch black as I stumbled over supplies lining the hallway, trying to escape the deranged spirit.

"Crap! I forgot my med cart," I muttered, and quickly went back, pulling it toward the exit. It kept getting stuck as I yanked it through the dark hall. The sounds of chairs shoved aside followed behind me. I pulled as hard as I could and the cart finally broke free.

I could hear something following close behind, and filled with terror of a hand grabbing me any second. I had to hasten to the exit beacon. Scared out of my mind, I finally made it to the double door exit. I pressed on the exit button to open the doors and nothing. I was to the point of beating the release but there was still no response from the magnetic locks. The locks on the door were hardened and stuck from years of non-use.

"Shit, it's not opening." I turned and saw a darker than dark shadow slowly wafting in my direction. A massive, opaque, cloud-shaped figure slowly floated towards me and began to coalesce into something familiar. It shaped itself into a four-legged beast. The same big cat crossed with a Great Dane hybrid-monster body having a human-like head. It crouched down on all fours, into an attack position, before disappearing behind a bed near to my medication cart.

I quickly turned around, knowing it was about to pounce on me. *Bang*! *Bang*! "Open the door, please!" I screamed, hoping someone on the other side would hear me and come to my aide.

Something else frightening appeared behind the bed – a long-deceased mental ward patient. He slowly stepped out with one arm to the side and the other behind him. This mad man was massive, having thick wide shoulders and a bull neck.

Suddenly it came to me like a flash of long lost memory. "Could it be? How is this possible?" I wondered. It was the lunatic from my school. I remembered in unmistakable, horrible detail.

"Come here," it commanded, again. "I have something for you," giggling, playfully, like a child. It moved closer, shoving old beds effortlessly out of its way. There was no exit. I had resigned that this was the end of the road for me.

I turned and banged on the door again in a desperate panic. That was when I heard another person behind the door say, "Move clear. I'm opening the door."

Instantly, I heard an eerie voice next to my face rasp, "Turn around." I closed my eyes. I didn't want to see it. My body was frozen but my mind was almost fried. I felt the presence behind me and I knew it had finally caught me.

The doors opened slowly as an amazing ray of light sliced the darkness, like Moses parting the Red Sea, in front of me. Two capable hands pulled me into the new section of the hospital. The security guard noticed the terror in my face. He cautiously shined his flashlight down the abandoned hallway toward the mental ward. We both heard a chair screech across the floor.

"Close the doors – now!" Without question, the guard quickly shut the double doors.

"What the hell were you doing in there?" he asked.

"No time to explain," I replied, as I rushed passed him to the emergency room just in time. The head nurse directed me to the correct trauma room. I handed the meds to the doctor to get his signature.

'Wow, that was close,' as I reflected on what I witnessed. There was no way I was ever going to repeat that new shortcut. The longer trip to the pharmacy was the no-brainer, so I spent that extra five minutes walking back through the basement.

Marcus, the night security guard, caught up with me. "Wait, brother, let me talk to you," he said as he rushed down the hall.

'Great! He's going to snitch on me,' I figured, as I turned to address him. Marcus was an older black man in his late 60's with a slim build. He was a retired police officer and worked part-time at the hospital. We would talk occasionally, but only in passing.

"Hey, what did you see in there?" he whispered loud enough for only me to hear him.

"Nothing, I just got stuck," I responded, playing dumb. This was a small hospital and gossip traveled fast. I wasn't about to tell him what I experienced.

Marcus pulled me aside and with all sincerity said, "Shit, I wouldn't be caught dead in that place. I heard all kinds of crazy shit happening on that second floor, especially the old mental ward. That area is so bad even the janitors won't cross those floors at night. I guess you got lucky," he mumbled on the way back to his post at the ED entrance.

When I got back to the pharmacy, I must have had this strange expression on my face because the pharmacist quickly questioned me. "What happened?" he asked.

"I got stuck inside the old ED," I jokingly answered.

"You went to the mental ward at this hour! Are you crazy? That place scares me during the day, so I can't imagine how scary it is at night. I know for a fact it's haunted. Everyone knows that, well, at least everyone on the night shift." I just smiled and kept on working.

The short hand marked the time for me to go home. I made sure to throw some salt over my shoulder and prayed to St. Michael, the Archangel, before I headed to the parking garage. Still scared, I made sure to walk the areas with the most light. I avoided any shadowy parts. My hands trembled uncontrollably as I drove home. With the memory of that lunatic's face fresh on my mind, I slept with the lights on.

From that day forward, I avoided the old emergency room and the mental ward. I still question what the death creature wanted or if it just wanted to scare me and see how I reacted. It took the shape of one of my greatest fears. Maybe it was to teach me a lesson… or did it want me to be late? Making sure the patient passed away before I brought life-saving medications? I'm not sure, but whatever the reason, I hope I didn't give it what it wanted. I learned that the dead are aware of the living. So, be careful when visiting a hospital and look out for the beast that hides in the darkness. It may follow you home.

CHAPTER 12
Don't Say Its Name (1998)

People say they love a good ghost story or a scary movie. Popular ghost shows introduce fictional and non-fictional elements. Some shows script in real demon names to incite their viewers, but they don't understand the ramification of their actions. I do. If a person, *anyone*, says a demon name – even just playing around, that evil received invitation into that person's home. I experienced this phenomenon myself while in college. Regardless of the entity, spirit, demon, poltergeist – whatever verbiage one uses to describe this non-human – each one has a name. With increased accessibility of World Wide Web postings and uploads, new urban legends are given life. YouTube quick searches or even popular movies can open doors to real demons.

My cousin, after many years, finally told us the *full* story about what happened one horrible night. When she first told us her story on Christmas day, she didn't mention the fact that she and her friends had summoned Henry one night using a Ouija board. At the time, it seemed innocent because they thought it was just a game. Unknowingly, she had invited the cat man into her house. Henry paid her a visit the very next day. Helen, now married with kids, gave us a stern warning, the same advice I am giving you: whatever you do, *don't* say its name aloud, unless you want uncontrollable evil in your house.

Don't Say Its Name (1998)
Living Dead Girl

AFTER WORKING AT the local hospital for many months, I was ready to expand my mental muscle. I moved to Austin, Texas where I would attend St. Edward's University. My first year there was pretty wild and Austin was too crazy for my taste, so I transferred to St. Mary's University in San Antonio, Texas for my sophomore year.

My time at St. Mary's University was not without paranormal experiences. I was asked to help many of my friends with their paranormal problems. Not everyone believed I could see ghosts, but that was cool with me. I wasn't in college to prove anything to anyone; I was there for the sole purpose of getting my education. If someone wanted my help, I would gladly offer assistance.

St. Mary's is an old university established in 1870 on San Antonio's south side. Since the school was so old, it had its share of ghost stories and urban legends; I guess most universities do. While at St. Mary's, I had joined a fraternity, expanding my circle of friends. Bob, my newest friend, was a tall, skinny guy born in Mexico. He was your typical frat brother and a staunch skeptic on anything dealing with the paranormal.

It all began when I explained that my aunt was a witch who dealt with spells and specialized in cleansing dark energy. Of course, this isn't something you casually share with people unless you must – this was such an occasion.

My frat brothers and I had this daily after classes habit of hanging out in Bob's room drinking beer and watching TV. Bob looked tired, restless, and agitated, at least more than usual. I recognized this type of restlessness in me… the expression of terror that keeps you awake all night. Whatever he feared, I would take it seriously. Bob waited for the rest of our friends to leave, except me.

Embarrassed, he asked, "Can I tell you something, but you promise not to tell anyone?" I turned to look at him.

"Of course," I answered. In a fraternity, keeping a secret is almost the hardest thing for a young man to do, but I was old school. I believed in honor and a man's word, so I promised.

He began to tell me about the night terrors he was experiencing. His voice quivered in fear, "I think something is haunting me. It's my ex-girlfriend, but here's the strange part – my ex-girlfriend is not dead," he explained, looking perplexed.

A *living* dead person was new to me. I'd never heard of someone being haunted by a live person. "Oh shit, you're serious," I gasped, as I sat down on his couch. "What do you see, and when do you see it?" I asked. I wanted to know what-in-the-hell could make a grown man almost cry in fear. Deep inside, I didn't want to know. The less I knew, the less likely the entity would attach itself to me and follow me to my dorm. The last time I tried to help a friend it took a toll on me, physically and mentally, so I needed to be cautious.

"Which girlfriend are you talking about?" I asked.

He responded while looking outside his window, "Her name is Gloria and she lives directly above me."

Bob was currently staying in a co-ed university apartment located in the area referred to as the outback. He lived on the first floor and his bed was next to a window that faced the wall of the next building. Most students walked the path between both buildings because it led directly to the parking lot. Anyone walking by could easily knock on his window.

The school marketed the buildings as apartments, but in reality, they were dorms. The buildings formed a huge "U" shape and the apartment doors faced a common open area. In the evening, people would open their door and sit outside to watch students amble up and down the walkways to their next lecture. The structures were fairly new, so I was surprised about a ghost.

"I just ran into her this morning while I was heading to class. She looked normal to me," I explained, as I grabbed another beer out of his small refrigerator. "Now tell me about the ghost."

Bob turned off his favorite show and turned to face me. "It's crazy bro'. She's disfigured and bloody. She has a huge slash across her face. You can see her jawbone when she smiles; it's gross. She's wearing a white blouse but you can't tell that by the amount of blood and dirt on her shirt. Almost like she dug herself out of a grave. Her left eye was blue, like from a huge bruise. Looked like someone hit her with enough force that it knocked her right eye out of place; it was horrible. Her hair had clumps of dirt with pieces of meat still attached to it. The scariest part was her huge smile and perfect white teeth, when we made eye contact. I'm in shock. This is horrific."

I could see his hand tremble as he further explained, "That mutilated woman waved at me with such craziness that all I could do was close my eyes and hope she would go away. Then she began to knock on my window again. I didn't know what to do, so I waved back. I turned over to ignore her, but she wouldn't stop knocking on my window."

"Knock, knock, knock. 'Let me in,' she cried out, from the other side of the glass. When I glanced at her, she would point with her bloody finger at the door, to let her into my apartment."

"What did you do?" I asked, as the vision of a macabre zombie got under my skin. "Did you let her in?"

"Hell no," he answered, without thinking. "I just ignored her and turned to face the wall, away from the window. Think about it? Would you have let her into your room? What am I supposed to do? Let her in? I don't think so. She's a zombie. Shit got even worse once she realized I wasn't going to open the door. She pouted her lips at me and started to cry outside my window – crying!"

"*Knock, knock, knock.* The knocking just got even louder. Then this eerie voice screamed and raged like a desperate woman, 'Please let me in. I love you.' Banging on the walls started and her howling got so loud I wondered if anyone else could hear her. She sounded like a wounded animal. Paced up and down the back of my building until the sun came up. This has gone on night after night. Sometimes she begged me to go outside."

"So did you go outside?" I asked.

He replied, "Hell no! Would you go? She's freakin' scary looking.

I'm exhausted, man. I haven't had a full night of sleep in a long time. She comes every night and taps on my window. It doesn't matter if I have someone over to spend the night. She always appears at the same time. So what do you think it is?" he asked, hoping for a quick answer.

I asked, "Have you played with a Ouija board lately or any type of spirit-summoning games? I know you don't believe in the paranormal, but I need to know." He sat down and thought about my question.

He quickly jumped up with excitement, "I know what it is. I watched *The Exorcist* with Gloria for the first time."

I responded, "So that's nothing special. Hundreds of people watch *The Exorcist* every day without anything happening to them. Why would it be different for you?" He sat back down and explained that after the movie he decided to do some research. Being a skeptic, he looked up the demon that mentioned in the movie and spoke its name.

At the time, I didn't find anything strange about his research. After all, we were just college students and research was part of our everyday life. I wanted to help him, but I wasn't sure how. I'd never seen this type of haunting. It almost seemed like the spirit had a vendetta against my friend. "Not sure," I said aloud. "I need to spend the night to see what we're dealing with… and what it wants." We grabbed some beers and worked on a plan.

Reviewing the situation, my dorm room was adjacent to his apartment. My building was exactly like his, except I stayed on the second floor. I hadn't experienced any paranormal activity yet, just the random drunk walking up the stairs. "When did she start to appear?" I asked, trying to piece together a timeline.

Tired of various questions, he asked in frustration, "Can you help me or not?"

"Yes. Let me ask my Aunt Nico. She's a witch," I answered.

My aunt is a witch in every sense of the word. If you could picture a real witch, that's what my aunt looks like in everyday life – except for the pointy hat, of course. She's about 5'1", a bit overweight with huge boobs, and wild, long, wavy black hair. Nico is a smoker so she has a deep, raspy voice and is missing some front teeth from years of smoking. Even though she is a witch, Nico tries to help people.

When she was a teenager, she ran away to the capitol of Mexico where she learned the dark arts. She was taught white magic from my grandmother, and from her years of traveling through the underbelly of Mexico City, learned the Mexican witchcraft culture.

"The 80s were the apex of the witchcraft culture," she explained. "There are several types of *brujeria* or magic. The most widely used is white magic which helps clean the dark energy from a person; not to be mistaken for green magic, which helps with healing. Red magic deals with love and luck. The most feared, black magic, is used to hurt or curse someone. For the spells to work a soul is required." Most time she would offer *el muerto,* the dead, an offering for a favor in return.

"The dead follow you and me," she would say. "Use them, and you can become a powerful witch like me. Ignore them, and they will make you pay." She explained that I was born into of a long line of people that practiced *brujeria.* Supposedly, my family is related to an actual *nagual* or *nahual,* a human being who has the power to transform either spiritually or physically into an animal form. In our family, the *nagual* always took the shape of a big black dog.

At the time, I thought my aunt was crazy, but would later learn how wrong I was in thinking this fake. I know it sounds crazy, but I can tell you for a fact, that witches are real and the magic they practice is no joke. There are things in this world that no one can explain, so if you decide not to believe me, do it at your own risk.

I called my aunt and she explained what the apparition could be. "Does your friend have many women in his life?" Nico asked. This was not as a question, but more as stating a fact.

I thought to myself, "I guess so. After all, we're in a fraternity," so I answered "Yes." I had no clue, but I figured it couldn't hurt.

"Did your friend call out a demon?"

Surprised by her question, I answered, "Why, yes."

She was quiet for several moments and then confidently said, "Your friend cursed himself. By calling its name, he invited the demon and it followed him home. Since the demon can't appear like a beautiful girl, it tries to trick your friend into inviting itself *into* his home."

I had so many questions, but only one came out, "Why does she appear like a zombie?"

My aunt answered, "Because it can't mimic a child of God, it tries to copy Gloria's image. That's why she looks the way she does." I was even more curious now, so I pressed her to answer the rest of my questions.

She answered again, "*El Diablo quiere acostarse con el.*" "The devil wants to sleep with him," she answered. The first thing I thought of was a succubus. "He needs protection. I can help," she added. According to my aunt, *el diablo*, the devil, takes the form of someone a person cares about and tries to seduce them into having sex with that persona, in order to steal their vitality. An invitation must be given willingly, that's why the Gloria persona worked so hard to get Bob to let her in the apartment. It's a trick. Once the demon is inside, it will feed on a human until it has their soul.

She said, "Tell your friend to be careful because he summoned a powerful demon. It wants to do him harm. Maybe an ex-girlfriend or a lover is trying to put a curse on him."

"What does he need to do?" I asked. Now I was worried about something more sinister pursuing my friend.

"There is something he's not telling you. You should ask him before it is too late," she explained.

My aunt Nico gave me a list of items I needed to gather before I could start helping Bob. The first task was to locate a roll of red string. It didn't matter where I got the string from, as long as it was red. Once I had the red string, I needed to dip it in holy water, then into vinegar for three days. Next, I needed to get a St. Michael's pendant from a church and get it blessed by a priest. After three days, remove the string from the vinegar and wait for three more days until it dried. To finish the process, I needed to take the red string and make a necklace, placing the pendant on it.

"Tell him to wear the charm every night and the devil will not bother him anymore." I heard her raspy voice laughing because she knew Bob had unknowingly placed a curse on himself. She chuckled again, "Tell your friend to be careful. Next time the advice won't be free."

During the next week, I had gathered the items my aunt listed. I hadn't stayed the night at Bob's place yet, due to mid-terms and previous engagements. Besides, I needed time to prepare for whatever was haunting my friend.

After I had made the necklace, I handed it to Bob.

He asked me in a confused tone, "What's this necklace for? Why does it smell so funny?"

"Don't ask. Just wear it every night before bed and it should protect you," I replied.

He took the pendant and put it on without any objection. "What does it do?" he asked.

"It protects you from the devil, so let see if it works tonight."

He smirked, like he wasn't sure if I was kidding or serious. "Bob, this is serious. Either you cursed yourself by calling the demon's name, or someone placed a curse on you. This necklace can protect you," I explained. Without saying anything, he nodded. I think he knew I was telling him the truth.

The next day he found me at the frat meeting place in the quad, "It worked! She didn't appear."

"Good," I replied. And I was glad. I didn't want to spend the night. The risk of a succubus attaching

to me was too great.

"So what was it?" he wanted to know.

"You don't want to know," I answered. I figured the less he knew about the demon, the better off he'd be. The last thing I wanted for him was to empower the devil with his fear; so I kept the information to myself. Once a person believes in other-worldly beings, they may unknowingly open a portal. I believe he had invited the demon by saying its name. I also think, deep inside, he knew what he had done.

Out of sight, out of mind would be the only way to make sure he was safe.

To this day, he wears that necklace and is still my friend after many years of adventures. What I learned from Bob was to never say a demon's name – no matter what. If you do, that evil thing can take on the form of anything or anyone you love.

I began studying the art of witchcraft from my aunt. My goal was to use it as a tool to fight against the unseen horrors that waited for me in the dark. Later on, I would find out San Antonio, Texas was the mecca of paranormal activity. This became abundantly clear when I decided to rent my first apartment off campus. If you learned anything from this story, don't say its name aloud – no matter what. That is, unless you want the dead to keep you up all night.

CHAPTER 13
Home Invasion (2000)

S OMETIMES CHEAP APARTMENTS just aren't worth it. During my university days, I lived mostly on St. Mary's campus, but one year I decided to find an off campus apartment. I couldn't afford anything extravagant, so I looked for something not so expensive in a shady apartment complex near the school. St. Mary's University is near Westside in San Antonio, an area known to be full of crime and impoverished areas. I loved it because it reminded me of my hometown of Oak Cliff.

Westside was a beautiful location, full of trees and local businesses, just what I liked. The place was within walking distance from school, so it was ideal for a person on a budget. There was an apartment complex in front of a fork in the road, forming a "T" shape. The old Woodlawn Apartments housed mostly low-income tenants: poor Latino families and students. The combination of residents gave me a bit more confidence in my decision to lease the apartment.

The architecture itself seemed to be a relic from the seventies, coated with a mundane paint job of brown and white. There were visible signs of decay and peeling paint along the framing, proof of years of neglect. Each front door faced the others and all shared a common area that fenced an old dirty pool, ringed by an assorted mix of old chairs. In spite of all this, I found the building charming.

On my way to the manager's office, I walked past some gangster-looking guys sitting outside their door. The pungent aroma of cheap marijuana smelled like a dead skunk. I'm sure they viewed any university students as a bunch of well-to-do punks looking for a deal. What they didn't know was that I was just like them; I didn't care what they thought. They stared at me as I walked by their space. I caught myself smiling when we made eye contact. "Crap, I should have been a bit more gangster," I thought, but it was too late. I speculated on their impressions of me as I nodded to them by raising my chin in their direction. They nodded back, accepting me as a local.

I considered myself gangster, given where I grew up. Once I became a college student, I lost all my street cred. Now I was one of *those* rich kids, minus the wealthy part, that the locals hated. I didn't mind, I felt I earned it.

After searching throughout the complex, I finally found the apartment manager. The manager was an elderly Hispanic woman in her late sixties, and she reminded me of my mother. Her name tag spelled out "Carmela," which is Spanish for Carmen. She was a serious looking woman wearing a brown dress and black flats. Her hair was strikingly black for her age. She wore thick eyeliner, purple eyeshadow, and blood red lipstick; the look worn by girls in a club. Carmen smelled of menthol cigarettes and mentholatum rub, reminding me Aunt Nico.

Carmen invited me in to eat and called me *mijo*, which meant son. I asked if she had any apartments available. She turned and looked at me.

"You're a university kid, aren't you?" she asked, with a questioning look, wagging her finger at me.

"Yes, I am," I proudly assured her. I followed her into a small office where she sat down behind an old wooden desk covered in papers and coffee cups.

"I don't like renting to university kids. All you do is throw crazy parties and cause me problems."

I quickly answered with, "Not me. I'm just here to study." Besides, I knew there were other students living here. I explained to her that I came from a poor neighborhood and I could relate to her. After what felt like hours, but in reality was only a few minutes of convincing, she decided to give me a chance.

"There are no apartments available, anyways. Least none that you would like," she explained as she lit a cigarette, asking if I wanted one.

"No, no I don't mind. Whatever you have," I countered.

"Well, I do have one apartment that just became available. But it's not ready yet. And I have to warn you, you might not want it," she explained, weirdly. She whispered, covering her mouth with her hand, making sure her husband couldn't hear her when her tone changed. You know, the kind of tone used when someone wants to warn you and doesn't want anyone in ear shot to hear. "The police just released the apartment, so we're still fixing up the damage," she quickly mentioned, escorting me outside.

"Wait? What, police? What happened?" I stopped her, demanding to know more.

"I told you, you wouldn't want it," she smiled, convinced I wasn't interested anymore.

"Can I see it?" I asked, not giving up. Carmen stopped and looked at me, and in frustration, threw away the remains of her cigarette.

"Alright. Let me show you the suite before I tell you the circumstances about the apartment." I agreed, and we started to walk towards the unit. Making our way past the same group of young men, we exchanged nods and half-smiles. Maybe those guys weren't as bad as the thugs from Dallas. I tried to convince myself that we could be friends. I still considered myself a street kid at heart. Carmen, with one look, made the guys go back inside their apartment.

"Stay away from those people. They're always up to no good," she explained as we walked passed the group.

"Great, the only people I relate to seem to be the biggest trouble-makers in the apartment complex."

She was fast for an old woman. I felt like a child following its mother trying to catch up to her pace. We crossed the middle parking lot and walked passed the crummy pool up to the second floor.

"Wait here," she said, as she walked into the corner apartment. She opened the door, and the smell of metal and bleach assaulted my nose. I could hear her talking to a work crew inside the apartment. "Okay, come in," she called out to me. I slowly walked in expecting a disaster. I had set my expectations set dangerously low, but I was happy and relieved with what I saw.

I found the inside of the apartment to be dark and cold, considering there was no air conditioning at the time. The workers had been patching drywall in the dining room; five small patches were still lacking paint on the wall.

"The carpet is new and the wall is repaired," said one of the workers to the property manager. They quickly gathered their things and moved to past me, not once looking at me. It was strange, like they didn't even notice me, like I wasn't even in the same room.

"What do you think?" Carmen asked me. Even though this was a one-bedroom efficiency, it was huge for the square footage. The apartment interior was ugly. The kitchen was small and had outdated appliances, but I didn't cook, so that was okay. I figured anything beats a dorm room and it was perfect. I didn't want the manager to know I was interested.

"You can have it for three hundred a month," she said. Without thinking, I agreed. It was dirt cheap, and with my part-time job, I could easily afford the rent. Then she gave me a worried look, like she was about to tell me my dog died. "I must tell you something before you agree to rent the apartment. It might be a deal breaker," she explained.

"What is it?" I asked.

Carmen stopped and looked me straight in the eye, "Someone was shot and killed here last month. You're the first person to view this apartment since it happened."

With unwavering certainty, I responded, "I don't care. It's a deal. Let's go sign the lease." We both walked back to her office.

"How can I say no?" my thoughts racing. "It's what I'm looking for... and why hasn't it been put on the market yet?" I tried to convince myself I made the right choice. I had to know what happened. "So what happened?" I asked.

Carmen looked at me and smiled. She took another cigarette from the pack in her purse, lit it and leaned closer, whispering, "Let's just say he wasn't a good person and leave it at that." I wanted to ask more questions, but didn't want to spoil a good thing.

I followed her comment with, "Oh well, it's mine now." I desperately needed my personal space. I had shared a room throughout my earlier semesters. That created considerable stress because of my talents.

I called my parents and my fraternity brothers to tell them. They all had the same questions: "Is it safe?" followed by, "Are you crazy?" In the end, they all agreed it was a good deal. Regardless, I had signed on the dotted line and the apartment was mine.

I slowly moved in, buying the typical college apartment essentials, like a futon and beanbag chair, along with instant Ramen soup and snacks. On moving day, I didn't have that much stuff, yet my brothers helped out; probably to curry favor with me. I had an apartment now *and* a cordless phone. It was the late nineties and most everyone was still tethered to landlines.

The fall semester had just begun, and I was preparing for my junior year. It was my first week, and I was settling into my apartment. There were four units in my building, two on the second floor and two on the bottom level; we shared a small pool. I hadn't seen anyone use the pool, even in the sweltering heat. Probably because it didn't look safe, which mirrored nothing was up to code in my apartment.

After catching some enticing, fragrant aromas of curry and spices in the air, I decided it was time to meet some of my neighbors. A group of six Indian students shared a ground level one bedroom apartment. They were law students and we talked all night. I thought the living arrangements were crazy, but they explained that they lived at home on the weekends and only stayed in the apartment during the week.

"So what happened in my apartment?" I asked. I thought it was some drug deal gone wrong, or something justifiable like that, but it was a mystery. I decided to ask other neighbors, as well, and they weren't sure. The previous tenant never really socialized with anyone else; but for sure, he wasn't a student. The university would have announced something like a rape or murder of a student; I certainly hadn't heard anything at school. Campus police usually sent out warnings to all students, including those living off campus, should anything present as a danger. I got increasingly curious about what had taken place in my unit.

My fraternity brothers were equally excited about my new place. I quickly began getting requests to borrow my apartment for random events. Some wanted a quiet space to study; others just wanted a place to hang out away from the university. As long as they kept my apartment clean, I didn't mind. I was hardly ever at my new home due to a full class schedule and working. Having someone there was a comfort knowing my apartment was safe.

I hadn't shared what happened in the apartment with anyone, but I started to get small complaints from friends getting creepy sensations. Some reported weird smells and cold spots when they were alone. Others reported feeling scared because it felt like someone was watching them. I honestly didn't feel anything, until one night.

I began to hear heavy footsteps outside my bedroom door. It wasn't every night, but it was frequent enough to bother me. I had a spare set of keys for some of my brothers in case they needed to get into my apartment, but they had to call first before coming over – so it wasn't one of them. Every night, like clockwork, precisely at three in the morning, I heard *swish, swish* as a person walked back in forth in front of my door. I'd call out, "Who's there?" and the walking would stop. It almost felt like whoever was there wanted to warn me.

The longer I lived there, the more frequently odd things would happen. My television would turn on by itself while I was in the shower, or it would be on when I got home from school. Again, it could have been explained that my friends forgot to turn it off before they went back to school. At first, I ignored this as paranormal because I didn't want to admit it was happening. That is, until one night a couple of days before Halloween.

My late night shift was over and the only thing I wanted to do is sleep. It was a hard day at work, and I just wanted to rest my bones. I collapsed on bed, shutting my eyes, and fell into a deep slumber. Out of nowhere, I heard a man yell, "Wake up!" in my ear so loudly that I jerked awake. I expected to find one of my friends in my room. Mad and confused, I looked around to find nothing but darkness. "What the fuck!" I was angry as I looked around. The realization that I was alone sank in, my stomach pitched. It was three in the morning, and I knew this – whatever it was – wasn't over yet.

Suddenly, the bedroom door slammed itself shut. I whipped my head around to see it close, and nobody was there. Surely it was one of my brothers… there was no other explanation. Confused and still half-asleep, I now feared for my life. I could hear the sound of footsteps on the terrace in front of my living room door again.

The stranger had returned and this time I heard him whispering, "He's in there, and he's alone." Immediately, I heard such vicious banging on the door that I knew I was in trouble. *Pow, pow, pow*. I fell out of bed looking for my cordless phone as the door continued to be kicked.

'Shit! That door looked cheap. They'll be in my apartment in no time,' remembering that I had inspected the door before signing the lease. Barely having presence of mind, I retrieved my trusty bat from under the bed and waited for he/them/it to come in. I started sweating and a nervousness dread caused my hands to tremble uncontrollably. Sitting up to get my bearings, I could barely swallow my spit. My heart was thumping loudly through my shirt. I realized this was a home invasion and I was trapped on the second floor with no exit.

The front door splintered open with an explosive *boom*. No way was I going to die tonight, not without a fight. I stood up and faced the bedroom door. My hands tightened around the bat, ready it to strike the first bastard that rushed in. 'They're going to regret fucking with me,' I resolved, as fear turned to anger. This badass was ready to battle.

I heard mumbling and screaming from the living room and furniture being shoved across the floor. This noise was followed by glass shattering while they trashed my belongings.

"Check over there," said the voice of a young man from across the kitchen.

"Hurry the fuck up," the intruders whispered as they made their way to the kitchen, chairs falling as someone kicked them away. I thought any minute now, they'll be in my room. I could feel their footsteps vibrate through my skin.

A loud scream penetrated through the door, as an older sounding voice asked, "What are you doing here?" and then *bang, bang, bang*. A horrific, blood-curdling scream came from the dining room as I heard "*NOOOOOOOO!*", and then another *bang, bang*. I heard the sound of footsteps running to the living room door, the door slamming shut, then, dead silence.

I wanted to investigate, but I couldn't move – I was afraid. 'What the fuck was that?' I wondered. Even more bewildered, I finally looked outside to try to catch a view of the thugs, but nothing. 'What the hell…' I put my ear to the bedroom door and there was still silence. Cautiously, I opened the door and slowly looked toward the dining room. Everything was quiet as I looked around into kitchen, but it was too dark to make out anything. Still trembling, I opened the door with my left hand, holding my bat in the right hand.

Everything inside was as I had left it, nothing moved or broken. "What the fuck?" Confused and scared, I looked around. Suddenly, a loud *ring-ring* came from under my bed. I jumped like a cat! "Crap!" Talk about bad timing. I answered the phone, "Hello."

A creepy, deep voice came out of the other side, like an older man. "I can see you… and your blue shirt."

"Who is this?" I demanded to know. Heavy, deep breathing came out as I repeated, screaming into the phone. "Who the hell is this?!" I got angrier at the thought of someone spying on me. This pervert didn't know I wasn't to be fucked with. My intention to hurt this person grew exponentially. It was like I could feel his voice breathe over my skin. He just laughed. The more I demanded he tell me his name, the more he laughed and smacked his lips, like he was licking the sound of my voice.

The perv slowly whispered into the phone, as though he enjoying mouthing every word, "I am watching you sleep."

Creeped out by what he said, I replied, "Fuck you! I'll beat the shit out of you, asshole. Don't you try anything!" I slammed the phone onto the counter and slowly peeked outside to see if anyone had been looking into my apartment. This should have been impossible, since I was on the second floor.

The horror of his words hit me when I realized I was wearing a blue university shirt. Quickly, I looked around the room, checking the closet and the rest of my apartment. Furious and confused, I looked around until I was satisfied no one had pranked me, but the caller knew what I was wearing.

The phone rang again. I thought about not answering it this time, but I was furious at the thought of a pervert stalking me, so I answered. "Who's this?" I yelled.

"It's Mom," a woman's voice replied, my mother. She said she couldn't sleep because she had a nightmare about me getting killed in a home invasion. She woke up and quickly called me. "I tried calling you, but your phone was busy, so I tried and tried until you answered. She explained, "I dreamed someone shot you and you died in the dining room. I got so scared." Her voice broke up as she on the verge of crying. My mother worriedly asked, "Are you ok?"

I didn't want her to worry anymore, so I said "Yes." 'How in the world did she know?' I wondered. I replied, "I am good, Mom. Go to sleep and I'll call you tomorrow." My mother and I share a special connection. She has this uncanny ability to sense my emotions, and distance doesn't matter. It's comforting to know our bond connects us, even today.

The next day, I went to the manager's office and demanded to know what actually happened. Carmen sat me down and explained to me about the strange older man who had died in the apartment.

"That *puto* gave me the creeps because he would sit outside his door in his bath robe and watch the kids swim. He claimed he was a student at the university. I think he liked boys," she whispered in my ear. "Well, that's a rumor I heard. And, supposedly, people say the local gangs killed him, but that's just apartment gossip," she explained, then asked, "You saw him, didn't you?"

"No," I replied, "But some strange things have happened. Last night, I thought someone had broken into my apartment."

"Last night?" she repeated in horror. "Oh, shit! That's the same night of the week that someone broke into his apartment and shot him in the dining room. He didn't have any furniture, so he was sleeping in the living room." Carmen sat down to take a breath. Finally, everything made sense. It was occurring again, like Groundhog Day, but that still didn't explain the phone call.

Carmen explained, "He was a sicko. I know this to be fact because he would randomly call his neighbors at night, until someone would *69 his ass. Then they'd report him to me. I was about to kick him out, but he was killed before I had a chance to confront him."

I sat down, to also take a breath. "Someone called me last night," I told her.

She gave me a look of assurance, "You're not the only person to complain of a pervert calling and hanging up at night, even after the person died. I guess he's still around," as she made the sign of the cross on her forehead, then walked back into her apartment.

I stayed for the remainder of the semester, then, returned to the dorm after more paranormal events picked up again. Nothing major happened afterwards, except for random footsteps and voices at night. And yes, I would still get random calls in the middle of the night by the same unknown male caller.

So if you're ever looking for a cheap apartment, always ask for the history and why it's so cheap. You never know, it might have the ghost of a sick pervert… the kind that likes to watch you sleep.

CHAPTER 14
San Antonio Ghost Tour (2000)

A N URBAN LEGEND remains a legend until one actually witnesses said paranormal event. I love San Antonio because of the culture and the people. In fact, San Antonio is saturated with a rich, tragic history of war, murder, and broken dreams. It's the perfect recipe for a haunting.

I was still attending St. Mary's University during my senior year in college. It was early spring. The weather was horrendously scorching already, especially in Westside. This is typical weather for south Texas and I had no plans to be outside.

I had just finished moving back into a campus dorm room after recently vacating that haunted apartment. This was the first time I didn't have share with a roommate. I was happy. I had good grades and my life was on course. Everything seemed to be going my way – for the first time in my life. I felt like I had a handle on my curse. No longer was I a victim to my talents because I was able to sort of control my abilities.

My younger brother, Edgar, was coming to visit me. At the time, he was just fourteen years old and although he was on the chubby side, he was quite tall for his age. This was the first time he would be traveling by himself, and grown up enough that I wouldn't have to worry – as much – about someone messing with him. I wanted to show him around my adopted city of San Antonio.

My goal was to teach him how to have a good time on a budget. I had left my part-time job to focus on my studies; therefore, I had no money to take him to Six Flags. Being an unemployed student with no job, or money, my options on how to show him a good time were limited. I decided to get a couple of friends and conduct a mock ghost hunt because it would fit in with the upcoming Friday the 13th. It was perfect and wouldn't cost me a dime – well, maybe a few dimes.

Before my brother arrived, I researched the most haunted spots in San Antonio. I found a list of locations that paranormal groups considered the most haunted. I didn't read the details, I just copied the list. Then I picked out the sites that were located closer to the university.

I planned to start this adventure by going to the most legendary spot in San Antonio, the haunted railroad tracks. Then we would visit a San Juan mission a short distance away, followed by the Chinese Tea Garden, and ending our night in the Comanche Lookout Park. It sounded like a good plan, and doing a ghost tour is not easy on a poor man's budget. My friends said they would chip in on beer and munchies. I still needed map to help us navigate through the outer limits countryside.

I asked my friends Odet and Miro to join Edgar and me on this low budget thrill. They were more interested in drinking beer and having fun, but agreed to join our expedition – just to make fun of me. Joking at my expense was a common occurrence, but since they were my fraternity brothers, it was okay. We took my jalopy, an old, forest green Toyota Camry. It was a generic ride that my parents had bought for me when I went off to college. The classic tan color interior had a matching set of the beer stains. It boasted a wide back seat that could fit five skinny students; therefore, I was both lucky and famous amongst my non-car-having fraternity brothers.

My little brother arrived on a bus from Dallas, so I picked him up and looked for a place to have lunch. We stopped to have lunch at Pizza Hut, since they had a cheap buffet.

"So what do you want to do tonight?" I asked him.

Edgar responded, "What? No parties tonight?" Edgar, like my parents, thought all I did was party – from watching movies about frat house parties.

"You got me," I said, "There is a big party, but we're not going. Instead, we're going to the downtown and go on a ghost tour."

He smiled at me and said, "You read my mind, bro'." I explained to him my plans for the night and he loved the idea. After lunch, I took him back to my dorm room to settle in and get ready for our ghost tour. Little did we know it was going to be such a long night.

San Antonio Ghost Tour (2000)
Part 1: Detours

OUR FIRST STOP was the Alamo. Not my idea, but my brother wanted to see it. I try to avoid tourist areas like the plague. When we arrived, we spotted a ghost tour already in procession. They were walking through the front of the old historic structure, so we decided to tag along. We had no money to pay for it, so we sneaked into the crowd to listen in. It was your usual hoopla and history stuff. In a word: dull.

Edgar asked me if I felt any kind of energy around the old building. I replied, "I feel hate and fear, but there too many people to get a good read."

I convinced my brother and friends to go visit the Menger Hotel, a short walk across the street. Of course, they all agreed. This hotel is located next to the Alamo in downtown San Antonio. A family friend who had stayed at the Menger claimed he had witnessed a ghost on the second floor. I didn't have any notes on what type of haunting had occurred in the hotel, but I wouldn't need any. I would know if something was present.

Watching out for management and security, we wove our way through the lobby, making sure we weren't discovered. As we walked up the beautiful wood stairs, I looked down to the lobby. It was everything I had imagined the view would be, and was like stepping back in time to the majestic Old West. On this night, I didn't feel anything in particular, we exited the Menger.

Looking around, we spotted the Gunter Hotel and decided to check it out. It was only a couple of blocks down the street from the Alamo, so it would be a short walk to return.

Once I entered the Gunter, I felt death emanating from the lobby area. The energy was familiar. It was like being in a fog full of pain. It's difficult to describe, but this overwhelming fear engulfed me. One thing you must understand about me, I feel energy everywhere, particularly in downtown San Antonio. This energy, especially around the Alamo, is like being in an ocean of sensations. If I feel a strong, unholy presence, I should worry, because whatever it is, it warrants an investigation. Usually I avoid situations like this, but I wanted to show my friends that ghosts are real, even though every bone in my body told me not to seek out this energy.

"Let's go to the elevators," I told my friends.

They wanted to get a drink at the bar, so they replied with a snarky, "Why?"

"I feel something dark," I responded. As I focused on the feeling, I was compelled to select the sixth floor. They understood by the expression on my face that I was serious. Stopping mid-stride to the bar, they turned to followed me.

We stepped out of the elevator into a well-lit hallway on the sixth floor. Something was pulling me to the end of the hall. Familiar energy came over me as I felt a young woman's aura. The smell of freshly cut flowers filled the hall. I obeyed the compulsion to stop in front of room 646.

"Here – it's here," I whispered to my brothers, who were huddled together like sheep. As quietly as I could, not wanting to draw attention to ourselves, I whispered. "She wants me to come in.".

"Maybe she has friends?" one of my friends jokingly suggested; but no one dared to smile. I started to lean in to put my ear next to the door. But before I even touched the door, we heard a violent forceful *Bang! Bang! Bang!* from the other side of the door. I jerked back just in case the door was bashed outward. Hell, we all jumped back in horror. Then we heard savage knocks on the door – three times – from inside the room.

"That wasn't her. It's something else!" I screamed, "Let's get the hell out of here!"

Without saying a word, we all ran, stumbling and tripping as we tried to escape to the elevator. The hallway seemed longer, different. The dark energy was powerful – not a woman, but something more primal. I could feel the entity following us down the hall. Luckily, the same elevator car was waiting for us. We pressed the ground floor button repeatedly until the door closed.

We heard an echo of a scream coming from the hallway as the car descended. Thankfully, I didn't feel the energy anymore, because whatever the entity was, it was powerful. Too close for comfort, we bolted from the elevator and lobby exit as fast as humanly possible.

"What did you feel, man?" my friends asked.

"Nothing. Let's just go." I didn't want whatever it was to follow us. So we decided to go get the car and head over to the railroad tracks.

San Antonio Ghost Tour (2000)
Part 2: Haunted Ghost Tracks

OF ALL THE locations I selected for the ghost tour, the haunted ghost tracks were my least favorite. I thought it was just stupid and lame and another urban legend, but my brother really wanted to visit this spot. Located south of the city, the tracks were on an isolated stretch of road. Just navigating the trip to the railroad tracks was unnerving. We had to drive through unfamiliar country roads in the middle of a moonless, black night.

According to said instructions, if one puts their car in neutral on one side of the tracks, an unseen force will push the car across the train tracks to the other side. To catch these ghostly hands, some type of white powder gets poured over the trunk deck and bumper. We stopped the car below the tracks, got out, grabbed the bottle of baby powder, and floured the back of my car. Jumping back in, I put the car in neutral. We waited.

'This will never work,' I thought, but I was wrong. Even with three heavy men and one obese man-boy inside the car, it rolled silently uphill toward the train tracks on its own. "No way," I yelled. Yet, the unseen force continued to push the vehicle across the tracks. And just like that, we stopped on the other side.

"You saw that, right?" I excitedly looked back at my compadres. We all got out of the car to see if there were actual handprints. I must admit, there were. "No way! This can't be real," I told my friends.

It was then we noticed another group rolled to a stop beside us. Four attractive blondes, same age as us, doing the same thing we just did. What luck? And, what were the odds there were four of us and four of them?

"Hey girls, did you get pushed across the train tracks?" They excitedly and anxiously affirmed. We quickly picked out one for each of us – yes, tacky – but it made the night more enjoyable. I heard a loud whisper while we were still selecting.

"Hey, Oscar, you take the fat one," they chuckled.

I whispered back, "Shut up, fools," trying not to smile.

We introduced ourselves and talked for a while. It so happened, one of the girl's sisters was in town and they decided to do a ghost tour, just like us. They explained that they attended the University of Trinity, another college located on the east side of San Antonio. One of my friends asked if they wanted to join us on our ghost tour. They quickly agreed and suggested we all get in one vehicle and see if the auto would still move; a solid test with a heavier load. In hive mind form, we all agreed.

After some maneuvering, we all crammed into my car. As snug as a tin of sardines, each girl was perched on a lap. Except for the big-boned girl who decided to sit on my lap – she was the exception. She kind of had to anchor a foot in the passenger well to sit. Of course, I was gentleman and asked her if she was comfortable for our crossing.

We positioned my car in front of the train tracks, and again, the car began to roll forward. It wasn't a light movement like before, but more of a jolt. The car took off up the hill, pushed by an unseen force. We got out of the vehicle and checked the powdered bumper and this time, we found more little handprints.

We asked the girls if they wanted to visit the old San Juan Mission that was a mile or so from this place. They agreed again – zero hesitation. We waited until they parked their car and then crammed back into my car as we made our way to the old mission. This had the makings of a great ghost tour.

San Antonio Ghost Tour (2000)
Part 3: San Juan Mission

SAN ANTONIO IS known for Spanish missions located throughout the city. The San Juan Mission was built in 1716 as a church, and later was occupied by the Spanish before Texas was even a state. The structure was made from local rock and mud mortar, adding to its rich history. Most missions were places to convert the local Indians to Christianity, usually by force. Many times, the mission itself was site of Indian massacres, leaving hundreds of people dead or dying; this one included. No wonder almost all missions have at least one ghost story.

When we arrived at the San Juan Mission parking lot and we were the only car parked there. It looked safe, being well lit, so we started walking to the complex. The mission had already closed for the night, but we still wanted to explore. A thin fog had settled around the compound, and the wind had picked up. We walked around the perimeter of the church.

Suddenly, the bright white mission appeared, like a ghost in the darkness. I hadn't felt anything evil or out of place; I was dead wrong. Something was watching us from the darkness. I had been distracted from worry about the safety of the girls. We decided to walk back to the car once we reached the edge of the property.

We had clumped together and wondering about the luminous building. That's when we noticed a man, wearing black monk robes, walking a huge black dog. He was too far from us to make out discernable details, especially his face.

"That's strange, who would be walking with a dog at this hour?" she whispered to me. I looked at my watch and saw it was about one in the morning. Trying to stay cool, I pulled her toward the car.

"Guys, let's go. There is nothing here," I said.

I was worried this was a more-than-meets-the-eye situation. We kept walking to the car. That's when we noticed the monk and the dog were suddenly standing next to the Mission entrance. We looked back to the spot where the monk and the dog stood a second ago and they were gone. To our horror, the monk was not a monk at all, but a headless shadow with red, glowing eyes where its head was supposed to be; the dog was a huge black void. Needless to say, panic set in and things got crazy.

"Where is his head?" someone screamed out. "It's the devil dog! Run!"

Everyone ran to the parking lot. We guys outpaced the girls, who were screaming for us to wait. I glanced behind me. The shadow had noticed us – and knew we had noticed it, before blending into the darkness of the doorway. Feeling guilty, we stopped for the girls to catch up. In the commotion, we lost track of the shadow. At a final glance, we saw that the monk and dog disappeared into the church.

Finally, we all squeezed into the car and quickly took off. "Did you see that?" one of the girls asked, as looking for reassurance that she had seen a ghost.

"Yes, we saw him," we responded.

"It could have been a janitor, you guys," one of my friends suggested.

Who knows, it could have been a ghost, but we had no clue what we encountered. Much later, we heard of a legend about a Spanish monk was killed in an Indian raid. Now he wanders around the old mission at night with his faithful companion dog.

San Antonio Ghost Tour (2000)
Part 4: Devil's Bridge

Any location with the word *devil* in it should be avoided. I knew this was common sense, especially for someone who can see the dead. Being young and stupid, I ignored my common sense, and instead, I listened to my liquid courage and visited the Devil's Bridge, anyway.

"Let's go to Devil's Bridge. Isn't that near the San Juan Mission? I think it's in the 2400 block of Ashley Road," Miro suggested as he drove down the street. It was close to our current location, so it seemed like the right location.

I needed a break. My legs were falling asleep as the girl on my lap moved to get comfortable. The bridge wasn't on my list, but it sounded creepy enough. In my experience, all parks are haunted, well, at least the ones I had visited. We parked near a row of trees with signage that read *No Alcoholic Beverages*. My friends had already finished their beers and needed a place to relieve themselves. Edgar and Odet got out and stretched their legs. Miro, being opportunistic, took advantage and stayed to talk to the girls. He pointed to a gap in the tree line, saying, "The Devil's Bridge, it's over there!"

Still shaken up from the mission ghost, the girls didn't budge from our sides. We made our way past the tree line towards an odd cement structure. It wasn't a real bridge, but more an elevated narrow strip of cement that was wide enough for one person. We agreed that it didn't look too treacherous, so we'd cross it.

We automatically lined up single file. My partner, the girl who sat on my lap, held my hand. No one in the group suggested otherwise, so everyone held hands as we made our way across. A thick fog had begun to roll in, covering the bridge and surrounding area, so there was no way to see the bottom.

"Let's go. I know you're scared," I said to her. I didn't want to admit it, but I was, too. My ability was extra-hyper, ultra-sensitive to the paranormal. We started to walk across slowly. I was focused on every step.

She whispered, "Do you hear that?" That's when we heard voices and faint weird laughing coming from the bottom of the river, like they were calling to us. It sounded joyful, like a bunch of children playing. We couldn't pinpoint the exact location because of the fog. It seemed like the sounds came from everywhere at the same time.

Mortal fear shot through me, I felt like my life was in grave danger. We reached the midpoint and the *only* way was forward. The image of a zombie's hands pulling me down into the bottom of the ravine ran through my thoughts. 'Just make it across,' I thought. The girl next to me squeezed my hand tighter, as if she too, could feel the energy around us.

I turned to look down into the fog. I caught a glimpse of something moving through the top of the mist, just barely hidden. It looked like the top of a bald head. I sped up my pace, pulling the human chain of hands across the small bridge. You could feel something in the air. Whatever it was, it was watching us... and waiting. The farther we shuffled across the bridge, the more the voices seemed to echo off the walls of concrete.

A full moon had appeared for the first time tonight and it lit up the fog like a white, suffocating blanket. Again, the head appeared, but disappeared as soon as I noticed it, but this time it was closer. I felt the slick sweat from both girls' hands. The stress of falling into the foggy ravine was all too apparent. When we had almost reached the end of the bridge, I noticed that thing had moved closer to us inside the cover of fog. We were being stalked.

I pulled the group harder to get across. Maybe it wasn't a good idea coming here with someone like me. I drew the dead to me like a moth to a flame. Any minute I expected to feel a hand grab my foot. After several minutes, we finally made it across. I took a breath and looked for the head; it was gone. That's when I noticed an outline of red eyes looking at me through the fog. It was a dismembered head with evil eyes, and it was looking at me with undiluted hatred.

"Let's go to the next spot," I suggested quickly. Something told me we weren't safe here anymore. We all got back into the car; nobody second-guessed me. I wasn't the only person who felt the evil energy at the Devil's Bridge.

What would have happened if it had reached us? The thought of falling to my death gave me shivers. Many people have died here, whether accidental or on purpose. It wasn't a good idea to tell everyone about what I witnessed, because there was no point in freaking out the girls.

Now I understand why it's called Devil's Bridge. I felt the same energy at this place that I felt on the 6th floor at the Gunter Hotel. Maybe it followed us, after all, and was waiting to strike. I needed to be more careful. I felt responsible for everyone with me and I didn't want the entity to hurt my friends.

It was two in the morning now, as we walked back to our car. Excited for more ghostly adventures, we made our way to the Chinese graveyard.

San Antonio Ghost Tour (2000)
Part 5: Chinese Graveyard

I LEARNED LONG ago, that respect must be given to the dead. Unless you want to anger the spirits – and if you do, they will try to get revenge. Never explore a graveyard at night. It's a stupid idea. You will offend the dead and they will follow you home.

The Chinese graveyard is a hidden cemetery inside the city limits of San Antonio near south Zarzamora Street. This piece of ground is supposedly haunted by the ghosts of Chinese railroad workers. What makes this urban legend creepy? The location.

My friend Miro was driving, for hours, it seemed. He swore he knew how to find the Chinese graveyard. At some point, we stopped in the middle of nowhere to refuel, get more beer, and take another pee break. And, our legs felt better after walking a bit since the girls were still perched on our laps.

We continued driving south on Zarzamora Street and stopped in front of a big gate built along a decrepit fence. Posted on the wall was a sign warning people to stay away. This was another place on my list that was considered more of an urban legend than haunted, or at least that's what I thought.

Miro got out and opened the gate, saying "Come on. Let's go inside." I had a bad feeling about trespassing; the energy felt wrong.

"Maybe we should skip this one," I suggested. Of course, the girls egged us on. Even Edgar wanted to cross the gate. I shrugged and signaled Miro. We drove my car inside the property, blatantly ignoring the No Trespassing sign. The path was well hidden amongst tall fern trees and unusually tall grass. The further we drove in, the darker and more foreboding the woods became. Besides our headlights, the only other illumination was sporadic lighting from a full moon.

The night was dry and sticky and the air smelled of moss. Shortly after creeping along the path, my car started to stall. "Did you fill the tank?" I asked Miro.

"Dude, it was working," he responded, confused.

"Kill the lights. I think someone is coming," I whispered. I sensed the energy changing. We all stayed quiet while looking around. It was so dark that all we could identify were trees, grass, and enormous shadows. The girl on my lap clamped onto me, hiding her face into my neck; I felt her heart racing. She was scared. Hell, I was too. I knew this was a bad idea, but no one listened to me. We waited a while and discovered nothing.

"I don't see anyone. What do we do?" one friend asked the group.

"Let's go," one of the girls whispered.

I yelled at my friend, "Let's go back! Put it in reverse!" I felt something coming our way.

He shouted back at me, "I can't. It's not working." Miro was a good mechanic and a very resourceful guy, that's why I selected him to join me on this tour. He got out to check the engine.

"Turn on the headlights. Let me see if I can fix it," he asked; I did so. "Pop the hood," he called out. That's when we noticed we had somehow traveled to the middle of the graveyard.

"Why didn't we notice this before?" one of the girls yelled. The graveyard was full of carved Chinese symbols and old crosses. And we just happened to be here? What a coincidence. Stress and panic spread inside the vehicle like an unwelcome fart. All the girls began screaming for us to leave.

Someone yelled out, "Hurry up! Start the car!" Everyone was on edge. I waved at Miro to get his attention.

"Get back in Miro, I think something is coming." We then noticed someone, dressed in white, walking along the tree line in our direction. Then we heard the voices and whispers. There was no doubt now – we were not alone.

"What's that sound?" as Miro hurried back inside the car. *Click, tick, click*. A high-pitched clicking noise arose from the trees. It sounded like someone was throwing rocks into a pile.

That's when we noticed a fog had rolled in. Like a cunning predator, it knew we had invaded its space. "Start the car! Start the car! Hurry!" we all shouted. The temperature plummeted inside the car – enough to see frosty breaths exhaled from our mouths. I felt horrible, oppressive energy coming from the tree line; my ears started to ring. The fog had almost reached the tires. Miro tried once more, desperate for the engine to turn over. *Click, click, v-room*. Finally the car came to life.

"Go! Go!" everyone screamed. He put the car in reverse, spinning the tires, the engine roaring. His only illumination to maneuver us out of the graveyard was the brake lights. We took off like a bat out of hell, as branches and tall grass scraped the car. At this point, we were screaming as we watched the fog follow us down the trail; I was so grateful Miro held it together. When we finally reached the gate, Miro rammed through it. I knew the bumper would be all but falling off.

"Keep going," we shouted. As we flew onto the open road, the gate slammed shut, as though closed in anger. After several blocks, we stopped and inspected my car. By some miracle, there was no damage. Numb, I knew everyone wanted to quit, but my crew said nothing. One of the girls admitted she wanted to go home. Things were just too scary.

But, we had one last stop on our list.

San Antonio Ghost Tour (2000)
Part 6: Comanche Lookout

MY FATHER ALWAYS told me regarding the paranormal, "Never fear the dead because they cannot hurt you, but fear the living, because they can." I always remember his words, when I put myself in dangerous situations. Sometimes people can be more evil than the most evil demon.

We headed to our last destination, the Comanche Lookout Park, located at 15551 Nacogdoches Road. The girls agreed to visit this old Civil War fort because of the rumor it was haunted by Indians and soldiers. I had never heard about Comanche Lookout before so I wasn't familiar with its legends. It was far from our current location and on the opposite side of San Antonio. It was quite late now, and we all were tired, but we couldn't drop off the girls alone.

We reached the park and the first thing we noticed was a massive tower, standing guard in the center of the acreage, like an out of place lighthouse. The path to it was a narrow trail that snaked around a small hill overlooking the city. Out of the dark, we noticed a beacon of light coming from the tower.

"I see the light. There must be people there," I said, feeling more secure about the situation. I was worried we might get robbed. The park was in Bexar County and known to be frequented by local gangs. I picked up a sturdy branch, stripping the leaves and twigs, in case I needed to defend my friends or myself.

We started walking toward the tower. The path was a lot longer than we expected and surrounded by tall trees and plants that could easily hide a man. At first, the tower seemed to be very close. All we had to do was follow this narrow path up a hill toward the tower. 'Easy,' I thought. Who was I kidding? Nothing on this trip had been easy for me. As we walked, we started to glimpse shadows that seemed to hide between the trees and grass, staying out of sight. This made us nervous and we intuitively stepped closer together.

One of my friends whispered, "Do you see that person following us?"

I whispered back, "Yes. Let's keep on walking." Thoughts of the opening scene of *An American Werewolf in London* danced in my head as we continued deeper into the park. 'Something is following us,' I thought, as I tried to remain cool. We kept on walking at a fast pace. That's when we started to hear a high pitch whistle. Not a musical whistle, but more like a signal type of whistle. We looked at each other at the same time, with the same confused look. Half scared and our decision regretted, it was too late to turn back. I spurred everyone on, hoping we would find people at the tower. I knew someone was out there in the dark, waiting for the right opportunity to attack us. This was a perfect spot to ambush us, so we needed to reach the tower fast.

"We're almost there. Come on," I urged. We had walked for about an hour and were nowhere near the tower. The further we walked into the park, the darker the path got. Now the only thing we could see was the path and a few beams of moonlight. That was when we noticed a person standing between two trees. As soon as he noticed us looking at him, he quickly disappeared into the darkness.

"What did you see?" I asked one of the girls.

"It was someone wearing an animal skin vest and war paint on his face, dressed as an Indian, right?" she answered. Freaked out now, we instantly regretted coming to the park at this hour. It was clear that someone else was in the park, and he was following us. Another sharp whistle came from a different area of the park. The reply was the sound of a strange birdcall, *chirrup, chirrup, chirrup*. There was more than one person stalking us and they knew where we were.

Fearing an attack, we quickly turned around and started to walk back. No one wanted to see the tower anymore – it was too dangerous. More sounds came from the woods; the same person was pacing us toward the parking lot.

"Stop, can you hear that?" I said. Screams came from the direction of the tower. It sounded like people being tortured. War cries, followed by crazed yelling, came from all directions. The girls looked desperate as they scurried faster down the old trail. It sounded like hell itself had descended into the old park. We reached the midpoint marker when we heard another animal call right in front of us.

Everyone froze, not wanting to draw attention to our location, listening, intently.

Now fed up with the stalking, we shouted, "Who's out there?" We had had enough. If they wanted to rumble, then let's get this done. The girls clinched our arms, almost in tears. No response came from the stranger.

Again, the park fell into a dead silence. A sharp whistle broke the silence. Out of nowhere, a loud pistol discharged, *pop, pop, pop.* We all ducked, seeking potential cover. I had been close to several drives-bys in my life and this was nothing like that. This gunfire sounded close, and oddly, at the same time, distant.

"Run!" I screamed. We ran back toward the car as fast as our legs could move us. I brought up the rear, making sure no one was behind us. This time the trail seemed shorter and we could see the parking lot was much closer. I took one last look toward the tower and couldn't see it, or the light, anymore. Now, it looked way distant, but moments ago we would have all sworn it was closer.

Not wasting time, we quickly got in the car and took off out of the park. Being shot at elevated our stress to a higher level, so no one said anything. I felt like we had witnessed something we shouldn't have. We had so many questions: Who was following us? Why was there a light in the tower? Who whistled at us? What did we hear? Did we just see an actual ghost of an Indian brave in the park?

At this point, I didn't care. I had had enough of the paranormal and called it a night. Edgar, Miro, Odet, and I decided to get some breakfast and discuss our crazy adventure. We dropped off the girls and walked them back to their car. I couldn't blame them for wanting an escort. We had witnessed many crazy, unexplained things.

My brother and I went back to my room to get some sleep. I would soon learn the night wasn't over for me yet. My energy was drained. I was beyond tired – fatigue had overtaken me. I was so tired I had forgotten to cleanse myself from bad energy, a mistake I would soon regret.

It was just past four in the morning by the time I had dropped off my fraternity brothers. That troll a of little brother was fast asleep on the only bed – a twin size, so I had to sleep on the floor. My mind kept racing as I was trying to fall asleep; something was bothering me and kept me awake.

Exhausted, I dozed off. Around six in the morning, I was awakened by something in my room. It was still very dark. There was not enough light to reduce the shadows in the corners, even though I strained to see them. Something had drawn my attention to a particular spot... a sound? That something was a scratching noise, and it made me focus toward the bottom of the bed.

I noticed two small hands grabbing the bed sheets; I reached for them. The fingers didn't seem real. They were more like four thin, shards with dried skin, barely stretching over the bone. I tried again to reach for the hands. I wanted to make sure what I saw wasn't part of some bad dream. The hands quickly disappeared under the bed, creating a wave that raised the sheets.

That's when I noticed a person *under* the bed. As soon as I saw his face, I was paralyzed. Was that because of some supernatural force? I don't know. All I knew then, was this grotesque face slid out from under the bed. Its wide-open maw seemed frozen between a scream and a frown – so gruesome, like it was in pain. Long, black, matted hair crowned the hideous face. Its eyes were black holes of nothingness. Horrified, I turned my head, I couldn't look at it any longer.

Like something out of my nightmares, he bounced across the room, leaping on me, like a wild animal. Unlike a wild animal, this Indian-like creature held a tomahawk aimed at my head. The room changed colors with every blow landed. I wanted to block the hits, but became paralyzed again. I was helpless and at this demon's mercy as it swung the weapon wildly at my head again, and again.

Anger was smoldering inside me. I started cursing at the Indian. '*Chinga tu madre!*' 'Get off me asshole!', I screamed inside my head. "I am not scared of you," I repeated aloud. The colors in the room sparked to blues, purples, and reds, as it landed on my head again. "Get off *pendejo*." The more I cursed, the more control I claimed. "You're not welcome here," I commanded.

The Indian demon seemed to vibrate – for lack of better term – at a frequency that skewed my thoughts. The screaming was animalistic and savage. The right hand had latched onto my throat in a death grip, the left still landing blows on my head. I could feel his anger toward me.

That's when I noticed a smell like old, decayed shoe leather, drawing my focus to his appearance. I saw rib bones and hips protruding from his body. The skin, stretched taut like a drumhead, was as white as baby powder, a stark contrast to the war paint covering his eyes. He had long, black, fine hair to his waist, creating a long black trail. It looked too long for him, and flew wildly as he jumped around. The crown matted with red clumps, which gleamed like a red rubies. An old bandana covered his forehead and a large brown and white hawk feather was tucked inside. He wore a blue, long-sleeve shirt, covered by an animal skin vest, and soldier pants, the type militia would wear during the Civil War. He seemed to be a malnourished, pre-teenage boy, comparing his frame to mine.

I could have easily overpowered him if I had had control over my body. As he swung his weapon at my head, I noticed tears coming from his eyes. There was nothing I could do to help him. He was so full of hate. I was saddened when I realized he was just a scared child – a demon, but still a child.

He stopped when he noticed I didn't react to his attack. He slowly stepped back, realizing how futile it was trying to scare me, or maybe he realized I had nothing to do with however he met his demise. His anger turned to sadness. Regardless, he stopped screaming and retreated to the bottom of the bed, using a series of unnatural, robotic contortions. I watch him blend into the shadows and fade away.

When he turned around, that's when I saw the back of his skull was missing. Someone had scalped him with a dull blade. Bits of hair still clung to his skull, and a small patch of skin held onto a chunk of flesh on his scalp. A soldier must have done this while he was still alive, judging by the expression on his face.

I wasn't scared, I felt sad. I got up, prayed for his soul, and went back to sleep. I never found out who the boy was, but I hope he found peace. I realized going on a ghost tour, as a person who attracts ghosts, is not such a good idea. If you're ever in San Antonio, make sure to visit some of its famous haunted locations. You never know, the ghost of an Indian boy might follow you home.

CHAPTER 15
The Hangman's Tree (2001)

NOT TOO MUCH scares me these days, but sometimes you run into things that are beyond fear. At our fraternity retreat, I experienced something that scared me to the bone. As a brother, we had many adventures with the paranormal. I believe most of Texas is full of paranormal activity.

This was my last year at St. Mary's University in San Antonio. It's one of the oldest Catholic universities in the United States. Being over 150 years old, ghost stories and urban legends are ripe for this picking; but those are stories for another day.

Every year it was tradition to have a fraternity retreat with my Lambda Chi brothers. Not only was this retreat tradition, it was mandatory for all brothers to attend, and that included me. Since I was a senior, and had "senior-itis" in every sense of the word. I had a girlfriend at the time and preferred to spend the weekend with her. Since I still cared about my fraternity, they got priority this last time.

Finding a location that would host a gang of men was always a difficult task. We often ended up renting an old farmhouse in the middle of nowhere. On numerous occasions, when there weren't enough rooms for all sixty of us, some of us would sleep outdoors. Weather permitting, camping out wasn't a bad idea. We tried to schedule the annual retreat during springtime to make camping out easier.

This year, we found a beautiful ranch near Bandera, Texas; it was located near a thick forest. On this particular retreat, we rented a fraternity brother's hunting cabin. The cabin was smaller, so most of us had to camp out. I was part of the planning committee tasked with finding such locations, so I had to arrive early and help set up the events and meal preparations. We were staying for two days – just enough time to discuss current events and settle personal issues within the fraternity. This was more like a leadership workshop and bonding experience rolled into one even.

I hated driving so I let my friends drive. It wasn't that I was a bad driver, I just didn't like to drive. Luckily, I had friends who didn't mind. The time from San Antonio to Bandera was about two hours, through beautiful country, but I still didn't want to go. If you ever been to southern Texas, 95 to 100 degrees Fahrenheit in the spring is the norm. Now imagine being isolated in the countryside and not fun. I'm not a camper and this was not on my bucket list.

I packed the essentials, picked up my friends, and headed to the assembly point. We caravanned all the way to the retreat location, just stopping for food and camping items. As we passed small towns in the Texas Hill Country, listening to country music to got us energized. I worried about my car making it all the way to the cabin. Up to this point, old green had never let me down.

The hunting cabin itself was about 130 years old, so it had a bit of history. There was a family cemetery on the property, a common practice back then. Generations would often bury their dead on their land, at least that's what John told us. The property belonged to one of John's family, so a few of the brothers had already stayed there. The cabin was primarily for hunters, who were going after game, such as deer and quail. Not me – first time to visit the hunting lodge. Even though the cabin had three bedrooms and a big living area, it was too small for our sixty-member crew. Once we got supplies set up in the cabin, a group of us began setting up camp, which was quite a distance from the cabin.

Inside the woods, stood a gargantuan oak tree. It was so wide, in fact, that it took a human chain of three men to encircle the girth of the tree. For all its majesty, I sensed a malevolent energy. My sixth sense picked up death and pain, but I could not pinpoint the origin. This worried me. 'Should I tell my friends?' I pondered. I decided not to mention what I had sensed. After all, half of the group was camping under the old oak. I was going for safety in numbers, or so I believed.

The sky had turned an ominous gray and red, indicating a Texas-sized storm was headed our way. The charged atmosphere flashed cracks of lightning that illuminated the countryside. The wind turned the trees into whistling flutes, accompanied by the percussion of thunder. Branches danced to the eerie melody; the forest seemed to come alive. We caught the sweet scent of cedar as fireflies disappeared and magically reappeared around us.

Even if it rained, the tree would offer some protection. Nonetheless, I couldn't keep my eyes off the old oak. I knew the tree had a story behind it, but there was something else that worried me. I would swear the oak was looking at us with its one dark knothole of an eye. It sounds crazy, but I had learned to trust my senses, regardless of how foolish they seemed. Not many things frighten me, but I was legiti-mately fearful of that tree. I needed to be brave for my friends. After all, what could a tree do?

We finished setting up camp and went back to the cabin for the evening meetings and workshops. Everything lasted longer than we had liked. Once the events were finished, those of us camping sandwiched into the back of John's pickup truck and headed back the campsite. The sun had dropped hours ago, making it hard to locate our campsite in the dark – even with headlights and a full moon. After finally locating our country crib, we worked on getting a fire started.

"We were fortunate… it never rained," I said aloud. We took that as a good sign. Right on cue, the winds picked up once more and blew a storm cloud across the moon, effectively blocking all ambient light. No one anticipated it would be *this* dark. I always assumed we would be able to see close objects, but that was not the case. I looked around – pitch black. I couldn't see anything, not even a finger touching my own nose. Panic and chaos ensued as everyone in our group scrambled to find a source of light.

The wind whipped so violently it was impossible to light the match. It felt like the temperature had dropped at least twenty degrees in a matter of minutes.

"Hurry, it's getting freaking cold man," one of the guys urged.

"Hold your horses, I'm trying. Just give me a chance," another person responded in frustration.

"Turn on the headlights!" a panicked voice screamed out of the darkness.

A voice from the darkness hollered back, "The truck won't start, the battery is dead."

"Call Chris to come give us a boost with his truck," replied another voice.

"Let's get this fire started first, then we'll call them," a flustered, but calm voice suggested. Meanwhile, I just sat on the ground drinking my soda, listening to the banter between everyone.

"I can't start the fire, and my flashlight won't work," a panicked voice shouted – to anyone who might offer help.

"Shit, what the hell's going on?" another voice shouted hysterically.

'Great,' I inwardly groaned, 'No one had the foresight to check their batteries before we made this trip.'

After several minutes, someone more clear-headed called another brother at the cabin. They explained that the only person with jumper cables went to town and wouldn't be back for another hour. We decided to wait and sit in the darkness, our backs to each other, just in case something tried to sneak up on us. The only thing left to do? Open our beers.

We waited in absolute silence, in pitch-black darkness. Impossibly, we began to hear strangers arguing from a distance. At first, it was just noise we couldn't understand. Then we heard it clearly.

"The tree is over there. Bring the rope!" said a gravelly southern voice from deep in the woods, blended with screaming and yelling. The accompanying laughter made me edgy, it sounded evil. Even in total darkness, I sensed panic spread among my friends.

"Do you hear that?" someone in our group whispered.

"Yes, who the fuck can that be?" someone replied. The voices of multiple trespassers got louder and louder as the minutes passed.

"No, I'm innocent," an unknown man cried out. This was followed by running and more screaming. In the darkness, we heard cracking noises from branches being broken and rustling leaves. This was really bad and we were caught in the middle.

"What the hell is going on?" we wondered, huddling closer. This whole thing felt wrong, felt off. I listened to the strangers argue.

Then one of the shouted, "He's over here."

"Maybe one of us should investigate," an unruffled voice suggested.

"Maybe you should, since you suggested it," another responded. Whoever they were, they should have been carrying flashlights. There was no way someone was running around in the darkness, especially in these woods. Immediately, we heard another bloodcurdling scream, followed by cruel laughter.

"They're hurting him," someone pleaded.

We heard a branch jerk and the creaking of a rope, followed by gurgling. The intruders had to be almost on top of us now, so I balled up. If someone discovered us, I didn't want them to grab my feet or arms, no matter how dark it was.

Snapping, one of my friends screamed, "Who the fuck's out there?" That's when everything became silent. We sat in the darkness waiting for a response. To our horror, the voices started again. This time, they were focused on finding us, getting closer to our campsite.

A sadistic, evil voice called out, "There's more over here. Get 'em."

We didn't wait. We all got up and ran down the wooded path as fast as we could. "Fuck the truck! Let's run to the cabin," someone screamed. I could hear my friends scurrying and tumbling down the only path we had to get around the oak tree.

The further we ran, the brighter the surrounding woods became. Suddenly, the moon was visible again. As we ran for our lives, we noticed a pair of high beams coming from the opposite direction behind some trees. It was Chris, headed our way to give us a jumpstart. We waved him down and jumped in the bed of his truck as fast as we could.

"GO! GO!" we shouted, frantically, "There're some weirdos in the woods killing someone." Chris was a huge monster of a cowboy from Pasadena, Texas. Chris was never known to have run from a fight, especially if he had the numbers with him.

"Fuck that. Let's go see who they are and what they want," he demanded.

"Let's go back and get reinforcements and guns. You never know, we might need them," I said. He reluctantly agreed and fishtailed off to the cabin.

Once we got there, everyone wanted to know what-in-the-hell was going on. We all blurted the story, "Crazy weirdos were chasing a man in the woods. We heard 'em talking and screaming. Then it sounded like they hung him. They started hunting us, too. We were running back here when Chris showed up."

"Let's go back and check it out," Chris suggested. He got everyone hyped up for a fight. We piled into the rest of the cars and went back to the campsite. Driving back, I couldn't help but wonder if we had let our imaginations run wild. So far, everything looked normal as we drove down the dirt strip.

Finally, we reached the campsite as Chris's truck illuminated the campground. It was still dark enough to scare the bravest of us, but each item was as we had left it. Nothing was strange or out of place. We didn't find traces of anyone pilfering our campsite.

Mack, who had driven over John's dead truck, shouted, "Give me a boost, Chris! I need to start the truck," as Chris continued revving his engine, effectively muting Mack's request. He'd seen too much to stick around, so he went back to the cabin. The strange thing is that the truck started without needing a boost. It was like nothing had happened; same as the campfire – easily started.

Chris joked, "I think you girls got spooked and ran. You must have heard a squirrel or a coyote."

"No way. The truck didn't start and we heard voices," I replied.

"Sure you did." The cabin crew started laughing at us for running away. Chris suddenly stopped laughing.

"Do you hear that?" he asked. Everyone stayed quiet and listened. From a distance, we heard screaming, followed by a loud buzzing over our heads. The massive tree shook and bent, as though an unseen force traveled up and down the trunk. A loud, ear-splitting moan emanated all around us. Chris whispered, "What the hell is that?" Then the laughter started. A devilish, evil laugh coming from a very dark place.

Without saying a word, everyone ran back to the vehicles and we hauled ass out of the campsite. We found the rest of the guys inside the cabin and John cooking.

"John, we just heard the strangest shit! We heard voices by that big ass oak tree near the main trail in the woods," the words tumbling from us.

"Oh, shit. You stayed by that old oak? Bro's, that place is haunted. At night, we sometimes see glowing orbs and hear blood-curdling screams coming from that direction. I can't believe you guys set up camp there." As we explained what happened, John gave us a history lesson about the old oak.

"It's an unmarked cemetery, fools. That oak was the local hanging tree for slaves and criminals. The dead were buried in unmarked graves around the trunk." According to John, the area had a string of mob lynchings that resulted in the hanging of several innocent men and women. "Man, I wouldn't stay near that oak tree. It's rumored that you can still hear the swing of a noosed body at night. There are always screams from that area… that's why we never go into the woods at night."

"Yeah, thanks for the heads up, jerk," I replied. He laughed and went back to cooking dinner. Even big Chris was freaked. I don't think he had ever experienced a paranormal event of such magnitude.

We unanimously decided to move closer to the cabin, next to the cows. Trust me, it was better than the woods. I learned a valuable lesson: always ask about the history of where you plan to lay your head *before* you decide to set up camp. You never know, it might be haunted.

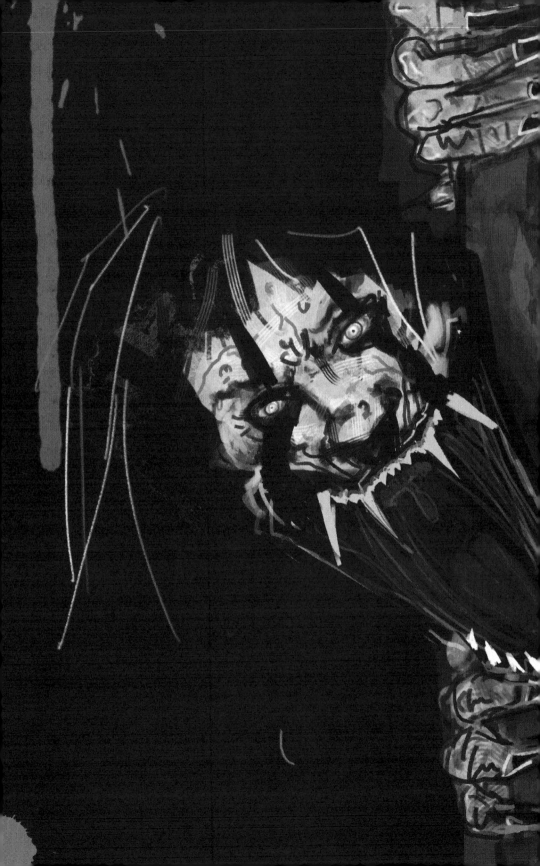

CHAPTER 16
Knowing (2000)

I T WAS MY senior year in college. I was more interested in finishing my education than anything else. Sometimes, I think my dedication to studying preoccupied my mind long enough to minimize the paranormal. Nevertheless, I was still haunted, but not as much. I knew that eventually, the dead would find me.

Because I was the first in my family to go to college, I strived to rise above what people considered an average ghetto kid. I relied on common sense to judge and handle situations, rather than emotion and violence. Sure, I still acted like a typical college student, but I had street smarts and something special; not wisdom, but more sixth sense.

As far as I can remember, I have been able to see energy, or what paranormal experts call auras. Many times, my sixth sense has warned me of danger, especially around people with evil auras; I feel and smell their bad energy. People with evil intentions usually have a black atmosphere surrounding them, accompanied with a stink of sulfur and rotten eggs.

My sixth sense also allows me to read people without talking to them. I can walk into a room and automatically read everyone's aura. This ability becomes useful when making friends because I can avoid those with evil intentions.

It all started when my friends and I visited the corner beer store next to the university. We were a party of four and had plans to hit a bar for drinks. We got out of my car to buy essentials: beer, gum, breath mints, etc. Before leaving the store, my sixth sense warned me of danger. I quickly looked around, saw my friends at the register, when I spotted thugs looking at us from the back of the store. Their energy was hateful and it radiated across the store, making my skin crawl. Things were about to escalate. I noticed one guy staying behind as the others were about the leave the store.

I quickly asked my friends to hurry up, and at the same time, keeping an eye on the gangstas' looking at us. Where I come from we, have a word for what they were doing to us – mad-dogging. Soon all the thugs crowded together in the parking lot. I could read their intentions and it wasn't good. All this time, my naïve friends had no clue what was going on; I did. I stated that we needed to move, now. As soon as we stepped outside, one of the gang members stepped up to us.

"Where you from, *puto*?" as he stood in front of the path to my car. His eyes locked on mine. He had that taunting, smug look – the kind of look that dared me to make a move. The street kid in me begged the logical me to beat the shit out of this wannabe gangster. I needed to be smart. This could turn ugly if I let it get out of hand, plus, I noticed a gun in one of the guy's pants.

'Of course they're packing heat,' I thought.

The gang of thugs formed a wall, blocking my car. I understood the situation and confronted the man. He was wearing a flannel shirt, a white undershirt, and baggy black pants. A red headband crowned his bald head, which was the canvas for a spider web tattoo. He must be the toughest one, judging by the rest of his tatts on his face and forearms. The ink that stained his skin was a collage of a young life lived too fast. Gallo looked even older than the others due to battle scars from previous fights. He was wearing large shades so I couldn't see his eyes. Even so, I stood my ground, cocked my chin, and nodded.

"What up, homeboy? We got no beef with you," I said, but he wasn't listening to me. He didn't respond to my question.

"Beat that prep's ass, Gallo!" a voice rang out from behind the man. *Gallo* means rooster in Spanish, and this *cholos* wanted to jump us or jack us up for our money. Either way, I wasn't going to let anything happen to my friends. Most of the locals thought all college students had money, thus making them an easy target. In reality, we were just as poor as they were.

The bad aroma of cheap Westside chronic came from every breath he took. That smell almost made me gag, as he stood inches from my face. I would swear whatever he was smoking was mixed with actual oregano. Being from south Dallas, I could easily recognize cheap weed. This was the kind of crap was sold by local dealers around the university.

His guard was down, not a very smart move unless he was just showboating. The street kid in me wanted to knock him out. By the way he was standing, he was practically daring me to hit him but I couldn't do it without making the situation worse. I needed to be smart and trust my sixth sense. His energy was different from his peers. 'He must be their *hefe*,' I thought.

The pungent odor of marijuana puffed into my nose as he yelled back to a man he called Spooky, "Calm the fuck down." He nodded and asked, "What up homie? Where you from home boy?" raising his hands in a challenging posture. He had a thick Mexican accent, sounding more native Mexican, than the Spanglish I was accustomed to on the Westside of San Antonio.

My first instinct is to notice everything I can, in case I have to give a description to the police. Second, is to remain cool, calm, and never show fear. People can sense if one is not willing to fight back, making for an easy mark. Third, I needed to show them I was also from the streets. I lifted my chin, while keeping my eyes locked to his, and nodded back.

"What's up homes? We're from the Westside, just like you. We just want to buy beer and look for some college honeys." I nodded back and smiled, trying to break the ice.

"Fuck that guy up," one of his friends screamed from the back of the group, trying to egg Gallo into a fight with me.

I looked into his eyes and said, "We got no beef with you or your friends." I reached out to shake his hand. He looked down at my hand for a second and shook it. Relieved, we grinned like two long lost friends.

"Where you really from, dog?" he asked.

"From Oak Cliff, in Dallas," I responded, trying to sound as 'hood as I could.

"No shit! My aunt and cousins live in Oak Cliff. It's cool," as he turned and made a parting gesture with his hands, "They're all right, let 'em pass," he called out to his gang of friends. All the men divided like Moses parting the Red Sea. My crew slowly passed through to the car, their eyes averted. Throughout, they stayed quiet as mice, not breathing or moving wrong to avoid a fight we couldn't win. After all, it was four of us, and seven of them and I am sure they had weapons in their car.

"You showed no fear. They could have beat the shit out of us, but you talked them out of it. And I am pretty sure they're your friends now. How did you do that?" one friend demanded to know.

"He didn't want to fight," I replied.

"How did you know that?" he asked.

"His tattoos," I responded. "He just got out of jail. I noticed a new tattoo with a date by his baby's face. I assumed it was either his release date or his kid's birthday. I know felons and they don't want to go back to jail. Trust me, it was all an act. He wanted to look hard in front of his friends. So when he realized I wasn't scared of him, he backed off. I'm sure he would have beaten me down if he knew I was scared." Satisfied with the answer, they stopped asking questions.

That night I trusted my sixth sense. The truth was that I read Gallo's energy. He had a blue aura, which meant he was a peaceful and happy person. I knew he didn't want to any trouble. I was right, but I couldn't tell my friends about this gift, unless I wanted to invite ridicule.

CHAPTER 17
Return to the Clown House (2001)
Part 1: Boy's Town

S O, WHEN MY father called and asked me for a big favor, I got a bad feeling. He wanted me to go to Mexico with him during spring break and help my aunt bring some furniture back to the states. My old man explained that cousin Mando and Aunt Maria would be riding with us. Maria was my dad's baby sister and had recently purchased a restaurant in the Rowlett suburb of Dallas. I loved my aunt, so I agreed.

Mando was about 19 years old at the time so, I figured why not, it should be fun. He was kind of crazy and was into the same things I liked. He had above average height and considered himself an amateur bodybuilder, so he was physically imposing. I figured between my cousin and I, we could look intimidating if we found ourselves in danger.

Curious, I asked my father what part of Mexico we would visit. Then I realized why my sixth sense went off. We would head to San Felipe and stay at my grandfather's old house. This was the same house where I experienced the zombie ghost clown many years ago, as a child. Immediately, I felt that same fright that I hadn't felt since I was a kid.

Thankfully, I had more control over my ability now, I was ready to confront one of my biggest fears in person.

If that wasn't enough, San Felipe had become a dangerous place due to the influx of drug violence. I had heard the rumors of cartel violence reaching the little town, but I was skeptical. Still, we had to be extra vigilant. San Felipe wasn't the same town I visited many years ago.

"Come, pick me up," I answered him.

"Good, we're a mile away," he said.

'Great,' I thought. I secretly hoped he was kidding.

They arrived at St. Mary's early in the morning as I finished my last class. We'd make the journey in a new black Ford F150 super cab truck my aunt just bought. Of course, my aunt put Mando and me in the back, just like we were little kids. I got comfortable for the 12-hour drive to San Felipe.

We arrived in San Felipe around eight in the evening. It was a hot, sticky night, and I could still feel the heat rising from the pavement. It all rushed back: familiar smells, like the gasoline fumes, exhaust from passing trucks, cooked chilies; music; sights of old streets and historic homes. The family *casa* looked the same, even though recently renovated.

My grandfather had rented the house to a family doctor named Kico. He was a family friend, enough that my father considered him a family member. The house had been converted into a small hospital, and my old room by the kitchen had been transformed into a morgue. The irony of the zombie ghost clown room being turned into a morgue blew my mind. Kico greeted us as he opened the front gate.

"Come in," as he greeted, helping us with our bags. Kico hugged my aunt and gave my old man a beer. He was still single, in spite of dating many young interns. I was sure he had a date tonight after catching the aroma of Ralph Lauren's *Polo*. My father would send him the signature green bottle every Christmas, his favorite.

Without giving him warning, I asked him. "Have you ever seen any ghosts in this house?"

He gave me a confused look and said "No," with an annoyed gaze.

"So, do you actually stay here?" as I blocked him from leaving.

"Of course not, I stay next door," he answered while changing the subject. I wouldn't let it go, so I pressed him to answer my questions.

"Don't tell me a big man like you is scared of a ghost," I goaded.

He gave me a pat on my shoulders, while grinning at me. Kico was a tall, slender man with a chili bowl hairstyle. He looked like a classic nerd that would pocket a pencil protector and wear high water pants. He was my father's age. They grew up together, but he never married. We considered him our crazy uncle, even though we are technically not related. I noticed he was dressed in a suit and smelled of booze.

"I was on my way to a party," the doctor explained, and asked Mando and me to join him. Shit, I would have gone anywhere just to stay away from this house. My sixth sense was going off like crazy.

'Stay here and relax, and tomorrow we can go out,' I thought. Too late, my cousin had already gotten into his car.

"Come on don't be a girl. I'm sure my uncle will let you go," Mando taunted.

"Okay, okay. Just for a little while," I reluctantly replied. I got in the passenger side of the little red beetle. My cousin tended to get crazy when he drank, so he would need to babysitter. The boozed look on Kico's face, blood-shot eyes, and slack smile was a clear indication he'd been drinking all day. I needed to keep an eye on him, too.

The VW bug bouncing along the stony street, Tejano music playing in the background, did not help my numb ass. We drove over small roads that were barely wide enough for one vehicle, zipping through small alleys and unnamed streets, towards the edge of town. I tried to remember all the landmarks in case I had to navigate our way home. On some of the old, small, white buildings with swing doors, I could make out *Cantina* and *Cerveza* in bright, colorful letters. What few lights there were, barely lit the streets, so most everything looked the same.

It was still early, so people were eating, visiting, and completing errands. However, the farther we went, the fewer people and streetlights we saw. I glanced at my cousin, concerned. He signaled that he, too, was worried.

We had been driving to the dangerous edge of town, where the streets become dirt roads and the signs disappeared. Up ahead, out in the middle of an alfalfa field, I noticed a building surrounded by a huge wall. We drove up to a big, red metal gate, complete with AR-47 armed guards, sporting cowboy hats.

We gave each other that look again, signaling, 'What the fuck did we get ourselves into this time?' No turning back now, I quickly looked around for an escape route – it was useless. Through doors of hell, we went headfirst.

This place was full of bad energy, so much so, that it I felt ill. It was too late – I was here, so I had better make the best of the situation. The compound had three structures, from what I could tell: a mansion, flanked by a hotel with an outdoor bar, and what was probably a guesthouse.

"Don't be scared, girls. It's cool, they're my friends," Kico explained. Yeah, right… So we all slowly unfolded out of the VW. My cousin and I towered over most of the people there, so it gave us a sort of false confidence.

A short, dark-haired, big bosomed woman came out of a room from inside the main house. She appeared to be in her mid-twenties, wearing a red, two-piece bikini that was way too small for her. With a wave of her hand, she singled out Mando and me to follow her. She gave Kico a hug and a kiss on the cheek. He whispered something in her ear that made the woman point at us, and they both laughed.

We were escorted to a huge pool party, the type I'd seen on MTV with a D.J. and bikini girls. I pinched myself. I felt like I had walked into a 2 Live Crew music video. The woman in the red bikini went into the hotel. Moments later, two beautiful girls from the bar followed her. One of the young women grabbed my hand and took me to a table with a tequila bottle already on it.

"Whatever you want," she spoke, in broken English, giving us this crazy wink.

"Bye, *chicos*," the red-bikinied woman said, waving at us. Both women followed her to the dance floor. My cousin and I sat down, as we watched Kico disappear into the bar crowd.

"Not too bad, right?" Mando asked. I nodded to placate him, but my sense of danger was in overdrive. From thin air, two more scantily clad dancers made their way to our table. One sat on my lap, while the other gave my cousin a shoulder massage.

"Are you hungry, sexy?" she asked me as she grabbed my inner thigh. Caught off guard, I forgot to speak proper Spanish and Spanglish spilled out of my mouth.

"Sure," I responded in a high-pitched tone. I awkwardly groaned.

"Ah, you American?" she asked. I couldn't lie. They both looked like they had stepped out of a *Girl's Gone Wild* video. Both women looked to be in the early 20's. The one who had spoken to me had an Asian face with long, black hair and blue highlights clipped in a Cleopatra hairstyle. What I noticed about her was the blood-red lipstick that shined like a diamond. Her name was Maria and she wore a tight, black mini dress, strategically held together by a couple of loops. The other girl wore a small crop-top with hip hugger jeans, adorned with a flower pattern running up each leg. She had huge hair, like something you would see in the eighties. Both wore platforms of six-inch heels.

"*Hola, soy Maria*," the Cleopatra/Maria girl whispered in my ear, as she sat next to me. Her voice tickled my ear, as I struggled to articulate a response. She laughed almost non-stop while making small talk, even though I couldn't hear her over the music. I couldn't help but stare at her hourglass figure. Her dress left nothing to the imagination. Being a gentleman, I tried to look away, but the more I tried, the more she placed her curvy bosom on my face.

I looked at my cousin, who nodded to go along with the girls. They were stunning, compared to us. I was puzzled why these beautiful girls wanted to hang out with us. Was it my college boy charm? Was it Mando's physique? We both wore rumpled jeans and t-shirts and were younger than anyone else. Neither of us expected to go out tonight, so we weren't dressed for such an occasion.

"Do you like me?" she asked as she played with my hair. I affirmed. She looked at her friend and they both got up and walked toward the hotel saying, "We will be right back, handsome."

"All the ladies are so friendly and grabby here, right?" my cousin asked me. We looked around and noticed a crowd gathering on the dance floor as the Mexican folk music blasted in the background.

"Whatever they bring us, don't drink it. I have a bad feeling," I warned him. My cousin agreed. After a short time, the girls came back wearing black, two-piece string bikinis that barely covered anything. With them, were two plates of tacos and two unopened Coronas. They sat on our laps again, but this time, they put their arms around us. Mando looked at me and raised both hands in confusion. I gave him a look of caution, to stay on his toes.

I felt Maria's soft manicured hand run up my shirt, as she kissed my neck. I looked at her and felt her energy. It was warm, sad, and scared, but overall, it was genuinely good. Her energy made me drop my guard and relax for the first time. I had nothing to fear from her. I could tell by the way she wrapped her arms around me that she felt something for me. That's the thing about being an empath. She couldn't lie to me because I could feel her actual feelings, and she was living in danger.

"Take me with you... to America," she whispered in my ear. I felt her heartbeat race after she laid her head on my chest. She looked like a lost puppy, her beautiful brown eyes. I lost myself in her gaze for a second, when a loud noise brought me back to my senses.

Abruptly, a bottle flew above our heads and broke behind us. We turned to look at the dance floor. Chairs and bottles started to fly around, hitting people as they danced. A huge fight broke out in the crowd near the bar. The girls jumped up as the fight spilled out toward us.

"*Perras, vuelvan para atrás,*" "Whores, come back," the D.J. announced over the music.

"Whores? What did he mean by that?" my cousin asked in a confused tone. That was when Kico stumbled to the table, drunk and bleeding.

"Time for us to go boys, quickly," he implored, running to his car. "You drive," throwing his keys at Mando. He dove into the back seat with the speed of a ninja.

Maria held my hand tight, "Don't go. Please, it's fine."

"Come with us. We can hang out somewhere else," I urged her, while watching a gang of overweight men headed toward us.

"No parada," she answered back. "This will stop," she explained. Her friend grabbed her hand and pulled her away toward the hotel. In a tug-of-war, I pulled her toward our car. I could tell she wanted to come with me, but her friend pulled her away at the last minute. I watched at her walk away as she put her black dress back on. She gave me one last look and waved back to follow her. Obviously, it was too dangerous and we needed to leave.

Mando ran toward the car and in mid-stride, said, "Wait – I can't drive stick." He looked at me.

"Don't look at me, I can't drive stick either," I replied. Fat old cowboys continued to bear down on us.

"Holy shit, let's go!" he said, trying to put the car into first gear. As it jerked forward, the gears grinding, we finally got rolling.

"Go, go!" I screamed. "I am not getting my ass kicked tonight, the first hour of being in this town," I asserted. My cousin had sweat dripping down his forehead.

"Hold on to something," he stated. Before leaving the big gate, I could see Maria and her friend pointing at us from the crowd, telling us to come back. I felt bad, like I was abandoning her. I think she really wanted to hang out with me.

As soon as we got onto the main road, we turned back to ask Kico for directions, but he had passed out in the back seat. After a several minutes later, he stirred and asked us if we enjoyed his gift.

"What gift?" we both asked at the same time.

"The girls," he answered.

"What? They were hookers?" Mando and I exchanged looks, asking, "And you already paid for them?"

"Yes, I did," Kico laughed at us.

"I'm turning the car back," my cousin suggested, but he was just kidding. "What happened? Why did we have to leave so fast?" he asked.

"No reason. I have to go to work in the morning," Kico said. "By the way, don't tell your parents," he said, passing out again.

"That's it! All that drama – for that?" I yelled. I thought of Maria, of going back. She didn't belong there, but I knew it was too dangerous to help her.

Besides, there was something worst waiting for me at home.

Return to the Clown House (2001)
Part 2: Demon

AFTER SEVERAL MINUTES of driving around lost, we finally located my grandfather's home. Kico made us park his car next to the apartment that was near our house.

"Remember girls, don't tell your parents," he said, as he went into his home. With all the excitement, I had forgotten about the house. My aunt had already claimed the downstairs bedroom, which was my grandfather's old room. The remaining bedroom was upstairs. Back in the day, no one dared to stay in this room. Not sure why, but it always gave everyone the creeps.

The stairs leading to the old second bedroom – my room – included renovations for a new bathroom and upstairs living room, providing a great view the town. Next to the living room were metal stairs that led up to the third floor.

Unchanged, was the third floor. There was a patio with a strung clothesline, in front of a single room closed by a metal door with a frosted window panel. Inside the room, a queen-sized bed and an old dresser full of clothes. How odd… someone leaving their stuff here: shoes, coats, and books – everything was covered by a layer of dust. Why leave their possessions? Although the room had a window, there was no view of the town or indoor cross-breeze, and no adornment of blinds or curtains. It was an odd place to put a window and I'm not sure why there was one. The stairway to the patio had a metal gate that separated it from the living room. The window in my room, however, was the only way to see the stairway to the third floor patio.

My old man was waiting for me downstairs, with my aunt, in the kitchen, drinking a beer.

"Let's all go to bed," my aunt suggested, as my cousin followed her into their room. We walked passed the kitchen where I had first encountered the zombie ghost clown. Relief came over me because I no longer feared this entity. I was so confident, that I almost wished it would show itself tonight. I was not a little kid anymore, so it couldn't scare me like it did so long ago.

As my dad and I lugged our bags up the concrete stairs, as my sixth sense tingled again. I felt an intense, dark energy – not human, but something more ancient. It was too much and it was all over the house. Maybe I made a mistake by daring the clown to show himself. My head was spinning. I was overwhelmed by this presence. Dad never let on if he sensed anything, or not.

We finally got our bags to the second floor. My father had tried to clean the room before I got home, but failed. The room was old and smelled of mothballs and dust. I placed my bags next to the bed. The mattress was hard and the sheets were dirty. No one had slept in this room for a long time. I chose the side of the bed next to the wall, away from the window. I had a bad feeling about the window. To tell you the truth, windows make me nervous. My old man slept close to the door.

"You're not a bed wetter are you?" he asked jokingly. I decided to sleep with my clothes on. The bed was old and it might have bed bugs, so I wasn't going to take a chance.

"Turn off the light, will you?" I called to him. The moment the lights were off, we noticed this glowing orb coming up the stairs, passing the frosted window. "Is it a car headlight?" I asked.

"It's nothing, just go to sleep." Again, the light passed our room along the stairs to the third floor room. This time, my old man wasn't saying much. He was just quiet and observing the strange light.

"Can you hear that?" he asked. There was a *tic-tic-tic* sound on the walls. I was too busy looking at the floating lantern outside our room, to pay attention.

"I don't hear anything," I whispered to him.

"Maria, is that you?" he called out. An woman's raspy, deep voice answered back with a long, "Noooooo." My father leapt out of bed!

"Who's out there?" he demanded to know. I could see my old man's demeanor change quickly from defiant to scared shitless. Neither of us replied as we waited, nervously. My heart pounded through my shirt as my legs shook uncontrollably. I suggested Dad turn on the lights. He got up, flicked the light on, and opened the door. The hallway was dark. "There's nothing outside see, now let's go to bed," and slowly turned off the lights, making his way back to the bed. He said it in such a way as to make himself believe in his own words, but we both knew something was out there. I scooted a little closer to my old man. I was terrified.

The floating light resumed, slowly making its way past the frosted window. We could make out the shape of a small hunched back woman with long gray hair, walk by the door window.

"Who the hell is that?" I asked my father. Again, without warning, he raced to turn on the light switch and look outside.

"Nothing, it's nothing. It must be the passing car headlights reflecting off the windows," he explained. We both knew it was bullshit, but we decided that was the most logical answer.

"Dad, turn off the light and wait until we see it again, then turn them back on as fast as you can. Let's see if we can figure out what is making the light." He agreed. He turned off the lights and we waited in the darkness.

This time, no lights appeared through the frosted window. We heard a *tic-tic-tic* of nails tapping on cement. Instead, we saw a light in the window that faced the hallway stairs leading to the third floor.

I screamed at my father, "Quick! Turn on the light!" I really had to satisfy my curiosity of whatever was generating that light. This particular window had no frosting so we could see whatever was visible. Suddenly, a hideous, bright green face appeared on the other side of the glass. We recoiled in horror. A disembodied, disfigured face of an old hag stared straight at us from the other side of the window. Its milky white eyes bored into us with intense hatred. The floating head looked like a witch's Halloween mask with long, matted gray hair falling in clumps over its face. The nose was long, pointed, and rubbing against the windowpane. When it noticed my father, its enormous chomping mouth displayed double rows of sharp teeth. My first thought was that it was part lizard, because of the green skin.

The night was swelteringly hot when my dad was trying to clean the room earlier. He had tried to open the window to let in air to circulate, but the window had been nailed shut. Still, he managed to pry it open a scant couple of inches to let in some breeze. The green demon had managed to squeeze its fingers through the bottom of the window frame. What scared us the most wasn't the demon's face, but rather its other arm. The other arm wedged itself through the narrow passage and contorted its arm through the small gap, thus stretching its long arm in our direction. We watched the appendage move slowly, contorting and clawing across the wall, like a spider clinging for purchase. The arm and fingers stretching was as grotesque as it was unreal. Black fingernails grew to longer than 4 inches, making that *tic-tic-tic* sound as it moved for us.

When my father turned the light came on, the arm retracted like the release of a Stretch Armstrong doll arm. If it weren't for him turning on the light, it would have gotten me. When the demon realized we saw it, it withdrew into the darkness. The look of hatred that she gave my father all but burned into his soul. *Tic-tic-tic*, her fingers tapped, slowly disappearing. It pointed its long finger at my father, gave him a mocking grin, and licked its lips with malevolent glee. My old man flipped. Without any regard for me, he made a wild dash downstairs to my aunt's room.

"Don't leave me," I screamed like a girl, following him down the stairs. We practically knocked down my aunt's door, rushing into her room.

"What the hell?" my aunt exclaimed, jumped out of bed.

"*La bruja,*" "A witch,"my father screamed. My aunt instantly became quiet. They both had this wild look of fear on their faces. Maria was a newborn baby when the *bruja* tried to take her many years ago. That night was the first time my father encountered the witch at his family's farmhouse on the edge of San Felipe. "It's back for us," my father repeated. My aunt grabbed my cousin's hand and wouldn't let him go.

"If it takes me, then it will also take you," my aunt told Mando. He freaked out, as the memory of the zombie ghost clown came back to him. He and my aunt visibly trembled.

"Stay quiet," my father suggested. He put his hand up to Maria's mouth to cue her for silence. I ran and locked the door, then sat next to my dad. *Tic-tic-tic* came from the hallway by the stairs. Everyone in the room stayed silent, not daring to make a sound.

"Do you hear that?" my father whispered. To be honest, I couldn't hear anything but my heartbeat. "She followed us," my father whispered. *Tic-tic-tic* came from the kitchen; it was getting closer.

"Let's pray," my aunt suggested. So we all got on our knees and started to pray. This was the first time in a long time I feared for my life. I knew that thing wanted to eat me. I couldn't imagine what it would do to a child. The thought of this made me pray earnestly – out of fear.

A loud wailing came from the hallway followed by more *tic-tic-tic* sounds. The image of spider-like claws crawling against the wall gave me an uneasy feeling. The evil thing circled us, looking for a way in. This bedroom had no windows, so it had no way to get in. I knew it was waiting for an opening to ambush us.

"Make a circle and hold hands," Maria demanded, as we all prayed, clasping hands. It was closer. I could feel it hiding in the darkness. We heard crashing objects in the kitchen, chairs scraping against the floor. The metal door shook and rattled as an unknown force passed by. The more we prayed, the more the screaming intensified. When we heard a final, prolonged scream was when it all stopped. It was daylight now and we hadn't slept one bit. How could we? I was too scared to close my eyes.

"Was that the witch you told me about?" I asked my father.

"Yes, I think so," he quickly answered. He gestured for us to be quiet again while he listened. "She came back for my little sister, Maria. Or, maybe she came back for you, or Mando," he explained.

My aunt moved closer to her son. "You stay with me one night and now the witch is back… not a coincidence."

"I don't think it was because of me. I guess it wanted you, son," my father explained.

"You might be right," I answered.

After leaving the house and getting some breakfast, we came back to find Kico waiting for us at the front door. He had a half-smile, almost like he expected us to say something. Hell, I recognized his expression because I'd seen it so many times at attending the university. It's the type of look someone gives when they can't remember what happened the night before, so he was kind of embarrassed to see us. Too excited to hold it in anymore, we told Kico about what we experienced last night. He laughed at us.

"Not you, too," he replied, almost like he knew what we were going to say. Kico quickly realized no one in our group was laughing with him. He explained that he rented the second floor bedroom used to house his medical interns to save the hospital money, and make extra cash on the side. It was the perfect solution, or so he thought, for any resident staying overnight.

This idea was abandoned when no one wanted to stay in the upstairs bedroom, anymore. *La casa de los muertos*, the house of the dead, is what the residents nicknamed the house. Soon, the rumors of the house being haunted spread amongst his medical students. Kico would receive frantic calls from his guests in odd hours of the night and find his residents outside sleeping on the street. His last student was the one who nailed the window closed.

"I'd rather sleep in the street than in that house," one of his interns complained. Supposedly, according to his students, anyone staying the night would hear noises and screams coming from the second floor. The one commonality was they all heard a tapping coming from the window, and the feeling of being touched while they slept.

"It was all crap," he proclaimed, "There is no such thing as a ghost. When will people grow up?" he screamed in frustration. Now I understood why he didn't want to answer my question when I first asked him whether the house was haunted.

"So why did you believe them in the end?" I asked.

He turned and with a straight face, said, "The strangest thing would happen to them. All of the interns would wake up with bruises on their body. So, I decided not to rent the room anymore. Do you believe that? What babies!" Kico laughed, as he looked at us.

"Where do the students stay now?" I asked expecting a smart-ass reply.

"Down the street about a block away, in your mom's parents' house. It's close enough, in case they're needed for medical assistance during the night," he answered. If only he knew… my mother's parents' house was also haunted, but that's another story.

My dad and I ended up sleeping on the floor of my aunt's bedroom with the door locked every night on this trip. We didn't experience the zombie ghost clown again, but we did see something a hundred times worse, the *bruja*.

The thought of that evil makes my skin crawl to this day. Knowing that the dead wait for an opportune time to reach out and grab you from under the bed, or in our case from an open window, is terrorizing.

The old house is now a hospital and the town morgue. I haven't been back to the clown house, but I do plan to make another trip to San Felipe. I finally understand why my father closes all his windows and doors at night because the *bruja* is real. I now wonder if the zombie ghost clown and the witch were the same entity. This entity would be one explanation for the increasing number of child mortality rates in this part of Mexico.

Returning to Mexico with my family wasn't just about helping my aunt, I wanted to find closure. On this trip, I ended up with more questions than answers. I discovered I was genuinely cursed, not by a witch or some kind of voodoo, but my own psychic ability. No matter what I do, the dead will always follow me, and the dead never forget. So be careful, the dead are out there, waiting.

Post Script

IMAGINE HAVING THE ability to see the dead, in a time when growing up and being different can get one killed. Follow his precarious balance dealing with the paranormal, dangerous gangs, college, and love life, during the early nineties. Oscar Mendoza's first book, <u>The Book of the Dead</u>, True Stories of Spirit Encounters, describes his paranormal experiences during his early years. This second book, <u>The Dead Follow</u>, continues Oscar's hair-raising stories about supernatural during his teenage years. The third book in the trilogy, <u>Los Muertos</u> will be released in October 2021. This will be his final book for more chilling occurrences with the unknown during his adult life.

Some of these stories are in production for cable TV episodes and a movie.

You can watch his ghost stories on:

- "Haunted Season 2, Born Cursed"
- "My Horror Story Season 1, Night Terror"

You can listen to his ghost stories on:

- *Snap Judgment: El Payaso Zombie*
- *Real Ghost Stories Online: Zombie Ghost Clown, Pig Man*
- *Unnormalparanormal.com: Book of the Dead*

One may follow Oscar's travels and encounters with the paranormal via these social media avenues and websites:

www.facebook.com/deadfollow   www.deadfollow.com
Instagram @thedeadfollow   Instagram @DallasGhostTours
                               or @dallasghosttour
Twitter @Thedeadfollow   Twitter @oscarmendoza

If you're ever in Dallas, craving a rush of adrenalin, Oscar's haunted ghost tour is waiting for you...

Made in the USA
Coppell, TX
18 November 2020

41576391R00127